A Profile *in* Purpose

Memoirs of an Appalachian Ministry
Two People – One Vision – Faith
Practical Action and a Farm

Mike Smathers

Copyright © 2023 Mike Smathers.

All rights reserved. No part of this book may be reproduced, stored, or transmitted by any means—whether auditory, graphic, mechanical, or electronic—without written permission of both publisher and author, except in the case of brief excerpts used in critical articles and reviews. Unauthorized reproduction of any part of this work is illegal and is punishable by law.

ISBN: 979-8-88640-929-1 (sc)
ISBN: 979-8-88640-930-7 (hc)
ISBN: 979-8-88640-931-4 (e)

Because of the dynamic nature of the Internet, any web addresses or links contained in this book may have changed since publication and may no longer be valid. The views expressed in this work are solely those of the author and do not necessarily reflect the views of the publisher, and the publisher hereby disclaims any responsibility for them.

One Galleria Blvd., Suite 1900, Metairie, LA 70001
1-888-421-2397

It is given to only a few to be the adventurers for God on the outer bounds of human order and progress and faith. Their service shall be for all mankind, and no matter how remote the community they know and love, the story will be worth telling at the reunion. And their reward shall be the joy of the adventure itself.

—Warren Hugh Wilson

Moses never reached Canaan, and here we will never reach ours, but the journey has been thrilling and worthwhile.

—Eugene Smathers

Most people see the world as it is, and they ask "Why?" He envisioned things that never were, and he asked, "Why not?"

(Words spoken at Eugene Smathers's funeral)

He preached his own funeral.

—Appalachian proverb

CONTENTS

Preface vii
Acknowledgments xi

Chapter 1   The Headline in a Footnote 1
Chapter 2   Gene and Loucile 13
Chapter 3   Welcome to the Real World 30
Chapter 4   "We Made It with Our Own Hands" 40
Chapter 5   "An Ounce of Prevention . . . A Pound of Cure" 57
Chapter 6   Puttin' Bread on the Table 71
Chapter 7   The Calvary Church Homestead Project 80
Chapter 8   The Scholar 89
Chapter 9   Race Relations Pioneer I 95
Chapter 10 Race Relations Pioneer II 103
Chapter 11 The Buzzards Come Home to Roost 121
Chapter 12 Farmer and Friend of the Soil 125
Chapter 13 A Living Laboratory 137
Chapter 14 The Lure of Greener Pastures 144
Chapter 15 "Great Day in the Morning" 154
Chapter 16 The Cumberland County Planning Group 160
Chapter 17 Sinners in the Hands of a Loving God 166
Chapter 18 The Road Less Traveled 180
Chapter 19 "Reflections in a Day of Trouble" 193
Chapter 20 Eugene Smathers Revisited 199

Appendix 1: The Radicalization of a Country Boy 203

PREFACE

HILLCREST CEMETERY, BIG LICK, TENNESSEE, JUNE 2, 2014: I am standing at Hillcrest, the Big Lick cemetery—standing next to a gravestone made from the native sandstone of Cumberland County, Tennessee. It is an unusual sandstone, occurring naturally nowhere else in the world. It can be found used in the Rockefeller Plaza in New York City, in the Senate Office Building in Washington DC, and in thousands of other public and private buildings throughout the United States.

The stone is soft and easy to work with when it is first quarried from beneath the ground. But it has two unique characteristics: one is its variety of colors, from deep brown to reddish to sky blue. The other is that unlike most sandstones, when it is exposed to weather, it gets harder rather than softer. Left in the weather long enough, it will achieve the hardness of granite or marble. Geologically, it is Tennessee quartzite, but it is more commonly known by its trade name, Crab Orchard Stone. This was one of the first gravestones in this cemetery to be made from this native stone. On a sloping side of the stone is written the name SMATHERS.

Next to the gravestone are two bronze markers. One is engraved "Eugene Smathers, Dec. 4, 1907–Aug. 16, 1968." The other has "Loucile Boydston Smathers, Aug. 13, 1909–Sept. 10, 1986" on it. The cemetery is slightly misnamed. While it is on a crest in a hill, it is not the highest crest of that rise. A quarter of a mile to the west, at the highest point of the hill and the highest point in the community, sits a small church composed of the same native stone. Beside the door to that church is a marker that reads, "American Presbyterian and Reformed Historical Site No. 123."

The purpose of this book is to explore some of the seminal events, ideas, and ideals that fill in those dashes between the dates and point to the connection between those dashes and that historical marker by the church door. This is a memoir. The sources of the material for this book were largely available only to the author (though some small bits of them are housed in the Vanderbilt University Library). Although the events, theology, and actions reported in this book are now four decades old or older, it is the author's contention that they still bear relevance to the contemporary reader. This is a retrospective account written by one who believes that this is history worthy of being preserved for posterity—even if that posterity be only a few people.

These stories and accounts are as true as the available written record or human recollection will permit them to be. Most of them are supported by written documentation in the Eugene and Loucile Smathers papers—letters, his daily journals, sermons, a parish newsletter, manuscripts, articles, and lectures he wrote or delivered, copies of which are still retained only by the author and his sister.

Some of the material is dependent upon other sources. Those sources are duly credited and footnoted in the text. Where the author thought it prudent or helpful, he has also footnoted some materials by Eugene Smathers (especially published material). Some footnotes are also used as a way of further explaining items in the text.

Some of the stories are from oral history passed along to the author by his parents and/or various other people of Big Lick, Tennessee, who lived the events with the Smatherses. Some are dependent on the recollection and notes of the author himself, who was personally present at many of the events and who has heard most of the stories, anecdotes, and theological discussions repeated dozens of times.

By way of full disclosure, it should be noted that some years after the death of Eugene Smathers, the author also served for ten years as pastor of Calvary Church of Big Lick, Presbyterian. That in itself is a unique story, but it is not the story told in this book. It also is well to note that said church continues as a vigorous and vital, though small, congregation and that the author still worships there.

Michael Smathers
June 2014

ACKNOWLEDGMENTS

This project has taken far longer than I ever imagined it would, primarily because of my health. The first parts of this story were written twenty years ago. I must express my gratitude especially to my wife, Judy, who has borne with me through all these years and proofread the original copy of everything that is written herein plus all those parts that ended up on the cutting-room floor. Also, to my sister, Patricia Smathers Konstam, I owe my thanks for reading much of the material, for all the advice she gave me, giving me honest feedback on what I should leave in as well as what I should take out, and what I should change. Sometimes it took both our memories to get the story straight. To Mary Ann Padgett, I also am grateful for reading some of the early drafts and giving me valuable feedback.

But above all, I owe a debt of gratitude to my parents and to others from the past generations of Big Lick, Tennessee. They reared me the way a village rears a child—with multiple sets of parents and lots of love. What I know of love I learned first from them. Beyond that, they helped to fill in the gaps in some of the stories and treated me as an adult from the time I was twelve years old. This meant that they told me stories and told stories around me that were meant for adult ears. It allowed me at twelve to start keeping notes that have now helped to shape this book.

There are, I hope, no errors of fact herein, but whatever errors there are can be credited to my account.

Michael Smathers

"Gene Smathers in his study – 1940"

CHAPTER 1

THE HEADLINE IN A FOOTNOTE

Everyone who exalts himself will be humbled, and he who humbles himself will be exalted.

—Luke 14: 11

PORTLAND, OREGON, THE CONVENTION CENTER, MAY 19, 1967: The 179th General Assembly of the United Presbyterian Church (USA) was in its second day. The new moderator (chief executive officer) of the general assembly had just concluded a news conference. The reporters present were a little confused about how to write their articles.

They got the facts straight enough. "Eugene Smathers won and William Hudnut lost."[1] That was the basic fact. They got it that Smathers was a fifty-nine-year-old native Kentuckian who had served only one church for thirty-three years. They got that his church had only seventy-five members and was located in remote Big Lick, Tennessee (pop. 300). They got that much of his ministry had been among the poor in Appalachia. Though he went out of his way to assure the reporters that "his people" were no longer poor, they seemed to conveniently forget that fact.

And they universally missed the headline although some of them had it buried at the end of their article or even in a footnote. Smathers's victory was a huge upset over the preassembly favorite, Dr. William Hudnut of New York, head of the church's Fifty-Million Fund building campaign.

Indeed, the 821 delegates, who had elected Smathers 462 to 359, had witnessed perhaps the biggest upset in the history of the United Presbyterian Church and its predecessors. Never in the twentieth century had the pastor of so small a church been elected moderator of the general assembly. Never before had the pastor from a mission church been elected to this prestigious office, and never before had the moderator of a general assembly simultaneously served as the chairman of a local farmers' cooperative.

Shortly after the election, a rumor began circulating that prior to the vote, only three people at the assembly had ever heard of Big Lick, Tennessee—one made the nominating speech, a second made the seconding speech, and the third was elected. While this was far from the truth, it does fairly represent the relative familiarity of the two names nominated for moderator.

Smathers was not the unknown that some made him out to be. His ministry, Calvary Church and the Big Lick community, had been featured in numerous publications ranging from _Social Progress_ to _Coronet_ to the _Progressive Farmer_. Even _TIME_, which had a reporter at the assembly, had featured Smathers in the Religion Section of its April 29, 1946, issue. That article, complete with pictures, had noted his pioneering ministry.

Smathers himself had published numerous articles and two booklets and delivered dozens of lectures, many of them multiple times. However, with a few notable exceptions, the distribution of his articles and lectures had been limited to small-town and rural churches and the organizations that represented them. Smathers had been a founding member of the Fellowship of Southern Churchmen. Though it was one of the South's first interracial civil rights groups, the Fellowship was a tiny organization largely unknown outside the South.

Over the years, hundreds of visitors from across the United States and many from overseas, people of different faiths and denominations, had come to see Smathers and his Big Lick parish. Few of these, however, had any connections to the higher echelons of the Presbyterian Church.

He had taught briefly at Vanderbilt University as well as at numerous institutes for rural ministers including many for African American pastors, but again these were limited to the South where the United Presbyterian Church had a very limited presence. Though he had once been offered a position in the national church office, an offer he declined, he had never served on any national boards, committees, or commissions of the church. Smathers was largely unknown among the larger Presbyterian communities in the Northeast, the Midwest, and on the West Coast.

One year prior to his election, he had consented to deliver a lecture on "How to be a Successful Pastor" at a conference of Cumberland Presbyterian pastors. He began that lecture in his usual self-effacing style:

> I approach the topic of this lecture with considerable "fear and trembling." Who am I to endeavor to tell others how to be a successful pastor, when none of the popular criteria of success characterize my own ministry? What business does one whose life and work have been buried in a small rural parish in the hills of Tennessee, whose churches are no larger than when he went there 32 years ago, who never has been and never will be an outstanding preacher, *who never has and never will hold any high-ranking position in his denomination*—yes, what business does such a person have, talking to you about what it means to be a successful pastor? (emphasis added)

Gene Smathers knew his place, or at least he thought he did. He was a lean, lanky, gaunt chain-smoker who spoke in a Southern mountain twang, identified with the derisive term "hillbilly." The suit he thought so expensive appeared slightly askew and out-of-date among the more nattily attired church officials and "tall steeple" preachers that accompanied him on the assembly stage. He seemed out of place among the denominational leaders and at the podium. He had spent his entire ministry in the little seventy-five-member church at Big Lick. His annual salary was little more than a shadow of his opponent's. His place, he thought, was with his little church and among the three hundred or so people of Big Lick, Tennessee.

On the other hand, the whole Presbyterian Church knew William H. Hudnut Jr.'s place. It was at the pinnacle of the denomination. Tall, urbane, and Princeton-educated, Hudnut's surname was honored in the denomination. He, his father before him, his brother, and his two sons all held or had held distinguished pastorates. His pastorates had been in Cincinnati, Ohio, Springfield, Illinois, and Rochester, New York. He was a member of the general council (the church's main governing body between general assemblies), the Board of National Missions, three other national committees or commissions of the church, as well as a member of the National Executive Committee of the Student YMCA, and the Boards of Union Seminary in New York and McCormick Theological Seminary in Chicago.

More importantly, he came to the assembly as national chairman of the Fifty Million Fund. This fund-raising effort was, at the time, the largest capital campaign ever undertaken by a Protestant church in America. He had overseen the overwhelming success of this campaign. He came to the assembly with fifty-three million in hand and another 1,500 churches yet to be heard from. The fund would eventually be oversubscribed by 20 percent. His report at the previous year's general assembly had brought the delegates to their feet, cheering and demonstrating in a style more typical of a political convention than a church conference. Hudnut's name was familiar to virtually every Presbyterian in the country.

When Hudnut was nominated for moderator of the general assembly, his election was considered a certainty. So certain of his election was the church-at-large that no one else had been nominated to oppose him; that is, not until four short weeks before the assembly. Meeting on April 11, 1967, the tiny presbytery of St. Andrews voted to nominate Gene Smathers.

Though he acknowledged the honor, Smathers tried to dissuade his friends and fellow presbyters from nominating him. They persisted, noting that this was the same day that his name was listed in the *Yearbook of Prayer* (a book that assigned each Presbyterian missionary one day a year on which his or her name was lifted up for prayer by the whole church). This caused one of the delegates to say to Smathers, "Brother, this is your day!" Speaking to the news media after his election, Smathers jested, "It was my day, all right, my *doomsday*."

The evening of his nomination, Smathers wrote in his journal, "Presbytery voted to nominate me for Moderator of G. A. (futile gesture) so I'll have to be the Commissioner." Even those nominating him did not expect Smathers to win. They thought this was an appropriate way to lift up Smathers's life and ministry for wider recognition throughout the whole denomination.

Three days later, April 14, 1967, Smathers wrote in his journal, "Presbytery has gotten itself a whale of a job by its action to nominate me as Moderator of G. A." A half-dozen people, Dave Campbell, Bob Helm, Harry Mercer in Tennessee, Arthur Tennies in Iowa, John Matthews, and Dick Comfort in New York, along with Smathers, geared up for the effort. They had to organize a national campaign in three weeks. They barely got a biographical sketch ready in time for publication in *Presbyterian Life*. They quickly put together a brochure that was mailed to all 831 general assembly commissioners.

They found a delegate from Atlanta, Georgia, Carol Payne, who knew Smathers well enough and was willing to make the nominating speech. However, two days before the assembly was to begin, they still did not have someone to make a seconding speech. The assembly was ready to open by the time they lined up Ira Sadler, an old friend of Smathers and a delegate from Nashville, Tennessee, to second his nomination. In spite of his misgivings and doubt, before leaving for Portland, "just in case lightning should strike," he told friends, Smathers wrote a short acceptance speech.

Awestruck, but not dumbstruck, Smathers set the tone for his moderatorial year in that acceptance speech. He first expressed his feeling by quoting the psalmist who said that he felt "like a pelican in the desert"—a feeling of one out of his element. But Smathers noted that the psalmist goes on to point out that "one within the power and purpose of God is never out of his element." Remarking that "the consolation in this awesome moment is that God must have had something to do with this, otherwise the impossible would have never become possible," he accepted his election as a call from God and pledged to do his best to fulfill the responsibilities of the office.

He went on to explore what purpose God might have in calling "one such as myself" to such a high office. He offers some "tentative answers," saying,

> Your call is no personal tribute. It is recognition of all those servants and members of the church who live and serve in the difficult places of this world . . . those who often face frustration and failure, who feel forgotten and alone . . . the thousands of 'little people' who sometimes wonder about their value and place in the life of the church . . . Because I believe this to be part of the meaning God would have us see in this 'impossible' event, it will be my special responsibility in the year ahead to convey the concern and care of the whole church to those who labor in difficult and often unrewarding ministries . . . those who are not often in the headlines."

He finds a "second meaning" in his election, going on to say,

> God is speaking a word about His concern for the poor . . . I dare see this meaning . . . because my whole life and ministry has been dedicated to bringing the Gospel of Jesus Christ

into a real and redemptive relation to people who lived in poverty . . . So again one of my purposes . . . will be to . . . strengthen and extend the mission of the church to the poor in America and the world.

> *I covet no greater privilege than to be the friend and advocate of God's little people, those whom Jesus called the 'least of these.'*

At a news conference after the election, Smathers was asked, "What do you think are the reasons for your election?" Smathers replied, "I don't know. I can't explain it. I don't want to say it, but something happened out there today." He attributed his election partially to the church's desire to "recognize those who serve in the difficult places of the world among the forgotten." Others at the assembly shared Smathers's belief that God's hand was evident in his election. More than one delegate noted that they felt a "Spirit" move through the assembly when Smathers was nominated.

Smathers had made one other decision before leaving for Portland. Should he, by some coincidence he could not imagine, be elected moderator, he would appoint an African American as vice moderator. Having spent his adult life entrenched in efforts for racial reconciliation, he continued to see race as one of the most pressing issues facing the United States. He would use the appointment of a vice moderator as a way of expressing his belief in racial equality. Accordingly, he appointed Richard E. Anderson, an African American pastor from Knoxville, Tennessee, as vice moderator.

Gene Smathers moderated what *Presbyterian Life* called one of the "great" general assemblies of the Presbyterian Church in the United States for its passage of the Confession of 1967, the first new confession adopted by the Presbyterian Church in thirty-three years.[2] In the year that followed, he traveled the nation and the world as the representative and ambassador for the United Presbyterian Church.

He spoke dozens of times at churches, church councils, and ecumenical gatherings. He presided over boards and agencies of the church. He wrote a number of articles for church publications. However, for that year, the office of the moderator of the Presbyterian Church was not in New York, but in Big Lick, Tennessee. Moreover, he kept his pledge to make a special effort to visit small and out-of-the-way mission stations across the United States and the world.

A fact unknown to any of those delegates gathered in Portland, Oregon, in May 1967, a fact unknown to Gene Smathers at the time, makes his service as moderator of the 179th General Assembly an even more remarkable story. The fact is that even as he was elected moderator, the chain-smoking Smathers was dying of cancer. He had been sick a lot—a lot more than usual—during the early months of 1967, but the cause of his ailments had not been diagnosed. When he was also sick during the general assembly in Portland, he blamed it on nerves, excitement, and fatigue. It would not be discovered until he had finished his moderatorial year in May 1968 that he was in the final stages of lung cancer.

He spent the last year of his life away from the people and places he loved. He survived a car wreck in Germany, the near death of his wife in Lebanon, numerous bouts of illness, and one of the busiest and most strenuous years of his life without anyone ever suspecting that he was seriously ill. He died on August 16, 1968, exactly three months after finishing his term as moderator of the general assembly. However, what makes Smathers interesting is not that his days after being moderator were so short, but that his years before assuming that position were so "full."

"Full" was a term Smathers used to define his own life near its end. It was a life consecrated by the Gospel of Jesus Christ and dedicated to the pursuit of a single vision. In 1940, Smathers wrote of his move to Big Lick: "I had come to remain as long as I could be of effective service in building a Christian rural community."[2] Adjusted from time to time as the world and his community changed, this vision remained the focus of his life and work. Periodically, he would update it and share it anew with his congregation in sermons entitled "Keeping the Vision."

It was a vision of a natural community transformed by the Gospel of Jesus Christ. The transformation would bring into existence a community that recognized Christ as the Lord of all its life, in which the church was at the center of all aspects of community life and in which every facet of the community's existence—land ownership, housing, family life, education, racial attitudes, or economic and recreational activities, as well as spiritual development—would be shaped and guided by Christian principles.

Pursuit of this vision resulted in a full life for one who was warned at the beginning of his life's work that he was wasting his life by taking a position at an unheard-of, out-of-the-way place in the hills of Tennessee. Organized and disciplined, he was a fine scholar. He had graduated cum laude and won the religious education prize at his seminary graduation. He was the only senior to graduate with honors in three subject areas. If he had only set his mind to it, he could have become pastor of a prestigious church, a seminary professor, or a church executive. But Gene Smathers had chosen a road less traveled, or perhaps it had been chosen for him.[4]

Though discouraged at times by frustration and defeats, and tempted at times by attractive offers to switch to a more prestigious and lucrative path, Smathers continued to walk the "road less traveled." He spent his entire professional career in one small community. In the end, he credited that perseverance with being a key factor in the accomplishments of the church and community he served. Near the end of his life, he answered those who had warned him he was wasting his life. He said,

> Maybe my life has been wasted, but it has been a joyful wastefulness. The life that was wasted has been full. Besides, perhaps that is what life is for in the economy of God, to be wasted for others.

"Gene Smathers in Moderator's Robe, Stole, and Cross – 1967"

"The new Moderator in a more typical pose – 1967."

NOTES

[1] *Presbyterian Life*, June 15, 1976, p. 18.
[2] Ibid, *Presbyterian Life*, 13 and 20–21.
[3] Eugene Smathers, *"I Work in the Cumberlands,"* pamphlet published by the Fellowship of Southern Churchmen in 1940. Also published in *Rural America*, American Country Life Association Inc., vol. 18, no. 7 (October 1940), 3–7.

CHAPTER 2

GENE AND LOUCILE

Homecoming
Love under the Lilac Bush

THE MANSE, BIG LICK, TENNESSEE, MAY 27, 1967: They met at the edge of the yard next to the lilac bush that they had planted together. He was returning from being elected moderator of the 179th General Assembly of the United Presbyterian Church. She had awaited his return anxiously.

They clung to each other, enfolded in each other's arms. No words passed their lips. None were unnecessary. Tears of joy glistened in their eyes. Gently, his lips pressed against hers. As she kissed him back, her arms tightened around him. They remained glued together for a long moment, and then, slightly embarrassed that they were being watched, they dropped their embrace and walked hand in hand up the path and into the house.

Three days short of their thirty-fifth wedding anniversary, they celebrated together. Words were unnecessary to express their emotions at that moment. The intensity of their affection hovered around them, all but palpable to those who witnessed their embrace. This was the woman whom Gene Smathers had pleaded with, begged, cajoled, and convinced to marry him thirty-five years earlier.

His words to her then—"I can never do my best without you by my side . . . Gee, sugar, with you by my side, I know we can do great things; without you, I'm really afraid"—had proved prophetic; she had, indeed, become the one indispensable person in his life. Marrying Loucile Boydston was the best decision Gene Smathers ever made.

She had been reluctant, hard to convince, but she had left home with this man. In the end, her love and respect for him (and perhaps her sense of challenge and adventure) overcame her general disdain for preachers, her low opinion of preachers' wives, her sense of unworthiness, and her almost obsessive fear of leaving home. This was the man she had worked beside for thirty-five years, and he was just now receiving the recognition and honor that she had long thought he deserved. There were so many bonds that bound them together.

Thirty-seven years earlier, they had met under different circumstances.

Rendezvous at Roger's Bluff

KINGSTON, ARKANSAS, AUGUST 7, 1930: Maude Basore Boydston is to be buried here today. The student intern pastor, Eugene Smathers, will conduct her funeral and burial. Her two young daughters, Dorothy and Charlee Loucile, and other members of her family will accompany her body from Berryville. And of course, there will be a few friends from Kingston who remember her from when she lived here. The oldest daughter, Ruth, will be unable to attend as she is away at a TB sanitarium.

They met that day, Gene and Charlee Lou, two lonely, heartsick people, each in his or her own way looking for a love that had been lost. He had never been so lonely. Kingston, Arkansas, was a dwindling out-of-the-way rural Ozark Mountain village. Most of the young adults had already left to seek their fortunes in a more upbeat locale. His primary companionship was with younger boys and older men. The only person near his age was the young schoolteacher, Emily Boydston.

They had become friends, but he missed his friends and the camaraderie of the seminary. Less and less, he also missed his girlfriend, Nora Lea Stamper. If the truth be told, the dying embers of his affection for Nora Lee only exacerbated his loneliness.

Their relationship had rattled along over the summer like a Model T on a mountain road. It had been up and down, smooth at times, rough as a rutted hillside road at other times. On July 19, Nora Lee had written him an uplifting letter; but by early August, Gene's affection for her was waning again. He had slipped into another blue and lonely funk. Today, August 7, his mood was even more morose because he had to conduct the funeral and internment for a woman he didn't even know. Having never conducted a funeral, he was stressed out about what he would do and say.

Charlee Lou had her own issues. Today, August 7, 1930, was the most miserable day of her life. She had thought that her stomach would never again hurt as bad as it had during that homesick semester at the University of Arkansas in 1928. But this was worse. Her mother's death had brought on a heartache that she thought would never let up. The youngest of three daughters, Charlee Lou had been the closest to their mother. She felt as low as she thought it possible for a human being to feel. She did not know how she would make it through the day.

She cried through the whole service so that she hardly heard the words of the lanky, loquacious Kentuckian who was conducting it. She did notice him enough that she asked her cousin, Emily, about this young preacher although she did not care much for preachers. She found most of them stuffy and boring. He noticed the brunette beauty sitting in the front row unable to control her emotions. He decided he would like to meet her.

When Charlee Lou decided to stay in Kingston with Emily for a few days, Gene asked her for a date. The next day, Saturday, August 9, 1930, they climbed Roger's Bluff together and looked out over the Kings River Valley where Kingston lay. It was a rendezvous they would never forget. They talked the clumsy parlance and moved ineptly through the awkward dance of the newly acquainted but powerfully attracted. Gene struggled internally with two conflicting emotions—his attraction for this new woman and his guilt over his wavering affection for Nora Lea Stamper. By the end of the afternoon, though he still did not know how he would ever tell her, he knew the romance with Nora Lea was over.

Charlee Lou struggled with her own conflicts. This preacher made the sun seem brighter, the future more promising, and her heartache less painful. Yet she was still in mourning, and she wasn't sure how she should act. She wondered what she would tell Dorothy about this young preacher. She had never met anyone quite like him. He was a college graduate and ministerial student, but without pretense, as folksy and down-to-earth as her cousin Emily. When they parted that afternoon, she knew two things: he was only to be in Arkansas for three more weeks, and she wanted to see him again.

Over the next few days, they exchanged letters; and on the morning of August 31, he motored into Berryville in an old open-seat Ford Roadster he had just purchased for the return trip to Kentucky and named the "Spirit of Kingston." They spent part of that day together. However, he had to leave in the afternoon so he could get as far as possible before dark because, as he explained to her, the "Spirit of Kingston has no eyes."

It would be the last time they saw each other for a year, but their relationship has clearly taken a serious turn. The next day, September 1, 1930, he writes her a letter from Doniphan, Missouri, that leaves little doubt about his intentions. Written on the stationery of the Grand Avenue Hotel, the letter says how much he misses her, that he is honest, that she can trust him, and that he will let his actions of the night before speak for him. He signs, "Just a blue and lonesome Gene."

Though he does not hints at it to her, Gene's blue mood is fed by more than the absence of Charlee Lou. Masked by his air of confidence is an unrelenting struggle with uncertainty about his future. Despite the summer's income, he is still broke and in debt. Not sure where he will get the necessary funds for the coming school year, he is considering dropping out of school. Even more importantly, he is in knots over the impending breakup with Nora Lea. Though he no longer has any romantic interest in her, he still feels a deep friendship that he values. Their continuing friendship, through a dying romance, will continue into October and beyond. Nora Lea will prove more influential than Charlee Lou in convincing him to return to school and more mature in facing their breakup than he was.

His promise of honesty and trustworthiness to Loucile was sincere and heartfelt, but he had made it knowing that he was not being truthful with either her or Nora Lee. Both women had letters waiting for him when he arrived home from Arkansas. Throughout September and into October 1930, he carried on correspondence with both women, neither of whom knew about the other. Twice he talked to Nora Lea, once by phone and once face-to-face, with the intention of telling her that his feelings and intentions toward her had changed. Neither time could he work up the courage to tell her the truth.

Nevertheless, she was perceptive enough to tell that something was different. After the phone call, she wrote him a friendly letter, urging him to stay in school and to stop smoking (advice he would ignore to his peril). She also wrote, "I had a funny feeling last night . . . seems like you wanted to tell me something and couldn't get enough nerve . . . If you realized while you were away that you didn't love me as much as you once thought you did, now is the time to tell me."

On September 18, after their face-to-face, she wrote him, "I was so glad to be with you, but I could tell there was something wrong—your feelings had changed—so . . . the best thing to do is give you a chance to tell me just how you feel about our friendship . . . I want you to finish school . . . just because your feelings have changed toward me & [you] don't love me as a sweetheart isn't any reason that we couldn't be friends . . . don't get blue."

In early October, he finally works up the courage to tell Nora Lee about Charlee Loucile and the end of his romantic feelings toward Nora Lee. The remarkable nature of their friendship is revealed by her last extant letter to him, dated October 4, 1930. Addressed to "Dearest Genie Boy," it is a friendly, encouraging, nine-page epistle. In it, she writes, "You have done the honorable thing in telling me your feelings toward me have changed and that you only like me as a friend." She asked him to continue writing and to call her whenever he is in Lexington. "Our friendship can never end as far as I'm concerned . . . Write soon dear chile [sic]." It is signed, "Your Pal & Buddie [sic], Nora Lea."

He still has not told Charlee Lou about Nora Lea. This final matter of this little love triangle was cleared up in a letter from Loucile dated October 20, 1930, in which she writes, "Wayne [Parker, one of the young Kingston boys whom Gene had befriended], just now told us you had a *girl*!!! He said you got special deliveries from her all the time you were here. He said he had seen her picture, [and that she was] prettier than I was [sic]." The letter is signed, "I Love You, Charlee Loucile." It is the first time that a clear expression of love appears in her letters. Gene and Charlee Lou's friendship had just turned into a romance.

It is destined to be a long-distance romance. As of October, 1930, Gene and Loucile have spent a total of two and a half days together. Over the next two years, they would spend less than two more weeks together before the week of their wedding. The remainder of their relationship rests on letters between them. They wrote often, sometimes every day, with seldom more than three days between their letters. Their letters would often cross in the mail, and then each would write immediately in response to the other's letter. Not all their letters have been kept, but those that have reveal how they built a romance in spite of the distance between them.

The fact that a romance can bloom and grow primarily through letters suggests that the attraction between the two is far more than physical. Especially is this the case in light of the fact that at least one of them (Loucile) continued to date other people regularly. Although Gene had broken up with Nora Lea, Charlee Lou continued to have several male friends and dated regularly during the period from September 1930–April 1932. In her letters, she frequently tells him some details of her last date. She asked him once how he felt about her dating. He apparently did not express any grave reservation because she continued to date. She worries that they have not gotten to know each other well enough and that he may be disappointed with the "real Loucile."

Throughout the school year of 1930–31, their correspondence continues on an almost daily basis. He called her on Christmas 1930, and they spoke on the phone. Then in the summer of 1931, Gene took an assignment in a Harlan County, Kentucky, coal camp. For whatever reason, none of his letters to her and only a few of her letters to him during the period May–August 1931 remain in existence. What does exist suggests that they continued their regular correspondence and that their love affair remained on an even keel. The few letters from that period that do exist make it clear that he told her some things about what was happening in Harlan County, including the fact that at one point he had contracted lice. It is also evident that Loucile was not entirely happy that he was in Harlan.

In late August 1931, before returning to school, Gene went back to Arkansas. They spent twelve days together. It was the longest time they would spend together and the last time they would see each other until the week before they were married. After his return to school, the correspondence picked up again. They write of their hopes, their fears, their dreams, and often of their "blue" mood and their desire to see the other. Sometimes they write something that does not please the other. She answers one of his letters by telling him that she did not like what he had written and that she was going to burn his letter. Nevertheless, she ends her letter by writing, "I Love You forever."

She occasionally expresses her distaste for becoming a minister's wife. Sometimes it is because she feels unworthy, but at other times, it is because she does not like most ministers' wives. In response to one of his letters in the summer of 1931 in which he describes a disagreement he had with the minister's wife in Cawood, Kentucky, she responds, "I bet 5 [cents] she is just about the kind of minister's wife I'd make—They are always hateful—I've never seen many I like." They discussed politics and theology some, and he would occasionally send her a copy of a sermon he had preached. The letters are almost always newsy, filled with great details of rather mundane events.

Although a great number of their letters still exist, it is not exactly clear what it was that kept their love alive and vibrant in spite of the absence and distance. It seems especially surprising in light of the facts that he had been dishonest with her at first and that she kept dating other men and was reticent about becoming a minister's wife. What is clear is that their affection for one another never wavered and, in fact, grew stronger the longer they corresponded with each other. This habit of corresponding frequently continued even after they were married. Whenever he was away from home for an extended period, as he often was during their thirty-six years of marriage, they wrote each other as often as possible, at least until the late 1950s when they got a telephone and could talk with each other when they were separated.

"Charlee Loucile Boydston Smathers – Date unknown."

Old Cupid Just Gave Us a Shove

Throughout the winter of 1931–32 and early spring of 1932, Gene and Loucile continue their almost daily correspondence. By April, his expressions of love for Loucile grow more ardent, and he begins to hint that he wants to get married a year sooner than they had previously planned.

However, one fact restrains him. While his desire to have Loucile with him as he begins his life's work is very strong, his search for a job is not going well. He considers graduate school (several of his professors urge him in that direction). However, he is broke and in debt. He sees no way he can afford graduate schools (although several graduate schools invite him to apply). He leans heavily toward a local church position, preferably in the National Missions field. As graduation nears, his search for a job grows more frantic.

On February 19, 1932, he wrote to Dr. Warren H. Wilson, superintendent of the Department of Church and Country Life of the Board of National Missions of the Presbyterian Church, USA (the Northern branch of the church). Smathers had been reared in and was still a member of the Presbyterian Church in the United States (the Southern branch of the church). But he was more than willing to switch branches. In fact, he felt more "at home" in the Northern branch.

He wrote to Wilson:

> As I have worked under the direction of your department for the last two summers, at Kingston, Ark. and Cawood, Ky . . . I am writing you in regard to a possible permanent location in one of your fields. I realize that the present economic situation is placing your work under a severe handicap . . . There is also the possibility that after my work last summer you would not care to offer me a place even if you had one. But because I have enjoyed working under your direction . . . I have decided to write you in this regard.

> I understand that you are to be here in March . . . But with only eight weeks remaining of the school year and as churches are to be scarce I thought I had better write before [your visit]. I will be glad to see you then . . . You know the type of work I was able to do and therefore my abilities. My work in Harlan did not seem to be considered much of a success by some people here in Ky., who have done their best to make it impossible for me to get a church in this state. [See Appendix 1] So far their efforts have not met with great success. My sympathies for the children and wives of the oppressed miners appears to be a dangerous thing. I do not know what the reports to you have been, but I feel sure that I can explain when I see you . . .
>
> Sincerely yours
Eugene Smathers
>
> P.S. I am willing to work on a minimum salary, if the field has opportunity for real service. I would prefer a place outside of Ky. As I have spent most of my life here and feel that the change would be for the best.
>
> E.S.

In his reply dated February 23, 1932, Wilson agrees to meet with Smathers, but is not very encouraging with respect to a job. "Opportunities are not many in the ministry now," he wrote. "Almost everyone is sticking to his job who has one, and the Boards are forbidden to do any advance work."

Nevertheless, Smathers and Wilson met on April 5; and on April 23, Smathers wrote Wilson again: "You will remember that during our conversation . . . at the Seminary . . . you spoke of a possible location . . . in Tenn. You advised me to write you before Seminary closed in regard to this place, and another possible place in the Ozarks."

On April 25, Wilson replied, "I [suggest] you write Rev. J. H. Miller, D.D., Lebanon, Tennessee, and say I suggested that you write him about an opening in the Presbytery of Cumberland Mountain this coming year."

Smathers immediately wrote Dr. Miller. On May 2, the day after seminary graduation, Smathers received a reply from Miller giving some details about the field that was opening up in Tennessee but not offering him the position. Later that same day, Gene wrote Loucile a long letter, which, among many expressions of love and of his need for her, information about his graduation and other news, told her of Miller's letter and its contents:

> I had a letter from Dr. Miller this a.m. about the place in Tenn.," he wrote. "He says they hope to place a man on the field by June 1st & that he was well pleased with my recommendations & would let me know in a few days what to expect. I asked him about the manse, & here is what he says, 'The manse is in fair condition. The back porch needs a little repair on the floor . . . .' He says, 'Ozone is naturally a pretty place—about 2000 feet elevation—a nice falls where the water plunges 70 feet to the head of a quite deep ravine. The East & West highway thru [sic] the state—concrete pavement—runs in sight of the manse. It has a railroad station. There is a P.O. there or you can have rural delivery from Rockwood, nearly ten miles away.' It sounds pretty good to me, how does it appeal to you, Sweet? I hope to hear something definite in a few days.

This letter also includes prodding for her to consider getting married soon. He begins using intermediaries in his effort to convince her to marry him. First, it is his friends. He tells her of bidding farewell to two of his best friends, both of whom were married: "Both of the girls [wives] advised me to get married [before going on the field] . . . [One] said, 'You'll not get lonesome no matter where you are if you have the one you love to live with.'"

He also tries to reassure her regarding her reservations about becoming his wife. He wrote, "Thanks, Loucile, for the gracious things you said about my accomplishments . . . [The fact is] the few things I've been able to do in the last two years I owe to you & Mother . . . You've been my inspiration, Precious . . . If I ever accomplish anything truly worthwhile in the future, it will be your love & you that are to blame."

He returns home in early May still without a job. He writes her on May 10 and again on May 11. She also writes him on May 11 complaining about it being so long between letters. His letter of May 11 is the only typewritten letter ever exchanged between the two. "Sweetheart, this letter may be the most fortunate one I've ever written," he types. "I am so excited I can hardly think, let alone write."

He then asks her a list of questions, all of which boil down to "Would you like to get married now?" "I can answer 'yes' to all of these questions," he types. "No one could love you more or need you worse . . . I got a letter today from Dr. Miller telling me I have been given the field in Tenn.." Then he turns to his next intermediary, the man who is to be his boss, typing,

> He wants me on the field by June 1st . . . He says it will be best for me to be married . . . We have already talked of marriage sometime this fall . . . You thot [sic] it would be best if we should delay awhile after I got located. Maybe you were right . . . But I feel that it would be best if we could be married before we take up the work. I *know* it will be best for me . . . If you are in accord with this idea that we be married soon . . . I could come to Berryville the latter part of next week, we could be married and get to Ozone by June 1st.

Later that same day, he writes her a second letter, this one handwritten, and turns to his third intermediary, his mother. He writes,

> I talked it over with Mother yesterday, and she felt [that immediate marriage] would be best for both of us . . . I can't tell you the fear that is mine as I think of going to Ozone to begin work, especially if I have to go alone . . . If I knew you were going with me, I could face the difficulties and hard

work ahead with a smile . . . *I can never do my best without you by my side* . . . Gee, Sugar, with you by my side I know we can do great things; without you, I'm really afraid.

At noon on Sunday, May 15, Loucile received the first (but not the second) of his May 11 letters. She responds *three* times on Monday, May 16, each time with a different answer. Early on the morning of the sixteenth, she sends a telegram saying that she could not possibly comply with his wishes to be married immediately. Later that day, she hastily writes a letter, saying, in part,

> I just sent you a telegram saying I couldn't possibly comply with your request, but now I've changed my mind (it's a woman's privilege, you know) . . . This is the hardest decision I ever made . . . I don't know if I can ever reconcile myself to leaving home or not . . . I'm terribly sorry I sent that telegram this a.m., but I hadn't talked to Dot [her sister] 'til noon today . . . [now she begins using her intermediaries, her sister and her sister's fiancé] I talked with Dorothy [Dot] and Manuel [Dot's fiancé] and they thot [sic] there was no use in waiting till fall . . . Don't hate me . . . You can't imagine what I've been going thru [sic], Sweetheart—but my love for you won me over . . . Don't hate me over that telegram . . . I am sorry no end. It wasn't lack of love for you . . . I was purely scared. I'm not now (not much).

Later that same day, she writes a second, slightly more controlled letter in which she changes her mind again. She writes,

> Yesterday at noon as I came from Church, I got your letter . . . I can't tell you how surprised I was at your suggestion that you come the last part of [next] week and me go back with you . . . I argued the proposition over pro and con . . . I didn't sleep any all night and feel terrible today . . . I sent that telegram in a big rush . . . I thot [sic] it best to wait awhile . . . At noon I talked to Dot & Manuel . . . We

had a family conference and I decided [to tell] you that I'd changed my mind and you could come on, but Darling, I know I have decided wisely in deciding to leave things as they are till fall . . . It's the hardest thing I ever did, trying to keep from crying when I think of leaving home . . . It was just too much of a leap to take so suddenly . . . Dot now thinks waiting is best.

Her reluctance is fed by more than her fear of leaving home. Although Loucile would later call herself "an Arkansas ridge runner from way back," that is hardly the way she thought of herself in 1932. She was not sure that she wanted to be a preacher's wife. Part of that is her insecurity. She is living a pretty freewheeling lifestyle for a small-town girl and thinks she may lack the necessary prim and proper decorum required of a minister's wife. Secondly, she fears being a minister's wife may turn her into something she does not wish to become. She had earlier written Gene about her opinion of minister's wives, saying, "They are always hateful—I've never seen many I like."

Beyond all that, for Charlee Lou, leaving home meant not only leaving her tight-knit extended family, but also her "club" made up of herself, her sister Dot, her four cousins, and her closest girlfriend. Although all were small-town Arkansas born and bred, they lived as a little cell of late-blooming flapper wannabes. They adorned themselves in flapper garb, danced the Charleston, played tennis and bridge, cursed, secretly smoked, went bathing in suits that revealed enough skin to be just short of scandalous, held down jobs, and lived independently. One of the great mysteries of this little story is how did Charlee Lou, the flapper gal, transform herself (virtually overnight) into Mrs. Loucile Smathers, the proper preacher's wife.

On the morning of May 18, Gene wrote an excited letter. He has in hand her first letter of the sixteenth (in which she says yes to his proposal) but not her second one of that date (in which she changes her mind). By the afternoon of the eighteenth, he has received her second letter of the sixteenth so he writes her a second letter. In this six-page letter, he accepts her apparently final decision to postpone their wedding until the fall. He goes to great lengths to assure her that he is not angry with her and that he understands and accepts her decision. But he has not given up entirely. He also writes, "Precious, now that this matter is settled, I have another question to ask . . . What time in the fall do you think we could be married? . . . Let us set some date as definitely as possible . . . It will be a great help to me, Charlee Lou, to be able to know at what date I will not have to live alone and lonely."

On May 19, Loucile writes that she is ashamed of her last letter of the sixteenth and then continues, "But I am asking you, if you love me, to forgive me for failing to respond to your idea concerning our immediate marriage—I feel that I have failed you . . . when you needed me most." Although she repeatedly writes of how ashamed of herself she is and how much she feels that she has "failed" him, she still maintains that it is best for her if they wait until the fall to be married. She then writes, "If I could only talk to you, I could make you understand . . . If I could see you this afternoon, I'd be the happiest girl in the world . . . *Damn it* I want to see you."

Gene receives her letter on the afternoon of the twentieth and responds immediately. He writes,

> Sweetheart, I feel as you do about our [lack of] success at coming to any definite conclusions about our future by writing . . . I've been so lonesome, have longed to talk things over with you . . . so when you suggest that you desire the same thing, your suggestion has a ready response. Yet you ask the impossible . . . There is only a week left before I must be on the field & I have many things which must be done . . . I have no money with which to do anything . . . all these things make it look sorta hopeless—but bigger obstacles have been overcome, maybe I can do the same . . . I wish I could assure you [that I can come], but I cannot . . . never forget that you mean all to me & that I love you with all my heart. Your own, Gene.

Four days later, to her surprise, he arrives in Berryville by bus at 6:00 AM. He explains in a letter to his mother written on May 25,

> I had a real nice trip to Berrywille, altho [sic] rather long and tiresome. [I arrived] at 6:00 [AM]. Loucile sure was surprised to see me and I was sure glad to see her . . .
>
> Loucile and I talked things over pretty thoroughly last night and she has decided to go with me. We will be married before long and will go to Ozone by bus early next week . . . We will leave here Mon. [May 30] spend Mon. night in Little Rock. Tues. we will go to Nashville, spending the night there. That will make us arrive at Ozone sometime Wed. [June 1] . . . I am anxious for you to meet Loucile . . . Lots of love, Eugene.

There is no evidence of where or how he got the money to get to Berryville and then back to Tennessee by bus. The most likely scenario is that it came from his mother's stash of "chicken and egg" money. (His mother would later amass enough to buy herself a nice car although she could not drive and never drove it. It was driven by one of her sons whenever he took her to church or to town.) Or perhaps it came in the form of a loan from his uncle Ulysses (his mother's brother) who had previously made him several small loans.

They were married by the Reverend B. N. Weaver in the First Presbyterian Church of Berryville at 10:00 AM on Monday, May 30, 1932, with members of her "club" in attendance. They left by bus shortly thereafter on their way to a place they had never seen. They spent their wedding night in Little Rock and went on by bus to Nashville where they spent the night at the Sam Davis Hotel that advertised "each room outside, with tub and shower baths, ceiling fan, and circulating ice water." Such was their honeymoon. The next morning, they boarded the bus, heading for Ozone, Tennessee, a place they knew of only from Dr. J. H. Miller's letters.

During their long courtship by correspondence, no truer words were written than those he wrote in one of his two letters of May 11, 1932: "I can never do my best work without you by my side." Not only did she return his love and keep him emotionally centered throughout his life, not only did she learn to endure the hardships of near-frontier living conditions, not only did she become his closest companion and compatriot, but she also became his most trusted advisor and confidant. As hardworking as he was, understanding and literate, she became his assistant in everything he did. She managed the church farm and church-initiated enterprises during his frequent absences. She staffed the health center during the times it was without a nurse. And she managed, virtually alone, the massive Christmas program conducted by the church.

CHAPTER 3

WELCOME TO THE REAL WORLD

The Ozone Years

JUNE 1, 1932: OZONE, TENNESSEE: It had been a short two-day journey, but once she set foot in Ozone, Tennessee, in midafternoon of June 1, 1932, Loucile Smathers, nee Charlee Lou Boydston, knew she was no longer in Berryville, Arkansas. Although a small town, Berryville had electricity and running water in most homes. Ozone was something else. There was no electricity or indoor plumbing. In fact, there was not even a good well.

Like Abram and Sarai, they had arrived at a place they had never seen before. What they knew of it had come from Dr. J. H. Miller's letter to Gene of May 11. Miller had described Ozone as

> naturally a pretty place—about 2000 feet elevation—a nice falls where the water plunges 70 feet to the head of a quite deep ravine. The East & West highway thru [sic] the state—concrete pavement—runs in sight of the manse. It has a railroad station. There is a P.O. there or you can have rural delivery from Rockwood, nearly ten miles away . . . The manse is in fair condition. The back porch needs a little repair on the floor.

He had included the following list of items that were supposedly at the manse: "Two beds, two washstands, two rugs, a piano, two dressers, a library table, a dining table, two small tables, one old rocker, three chairs, one stove heater, one buffet, and two mattresses."

Ozone did have a beautiful waterfall, but most of the houses in the community could best be described as shacks. Moreover, the manse was not as had been described. In fact, it was in such run-down condition that it was uninhabitable. Loucile described it in a letter. The furnishings, she wrote, consisted of "two old mattresses which had the appearance of being filled with bricks, a dining table, 3 broken chairs, library table, a dresser and numerous wash stands." The Smatherses were largely on their own and without any money. Loucile's letter continued, "We were compelled to establish headquarters at the 'village boardin [sic] house.'" They lived in the boarding house or in a small vacant house at Jewett (one of the other communities in the parish) until the manse could be put into livable condition.

However, the people were friendly enough. In the above noted letter, Loucile explained,

> The folk of Ozone gave us a "most royal" welcome, the whole country side gathered together for the occasion, some walking as far as six miles (not so much to satisfy their curiosity as to satisfy their thirst), the custom being to initiate each newly married man into his "state of bless" by a ceremony known as a "serenade" [or "shivaree," as it was more commonly known]. The men bring their stringed instruments and a rail. After playing and singing a few mountain ballads, the groom is faced with the alternative of riding that rail or buying each person present a bottle of "pop." The groom in question, considering it beneath his ministerial dignity to ride a rail, managed to raise the price of fifty-three bottled Coca Colas. Such was our introduction into the customs of the Tennessee Highlanders.

After the serenade/shivaree, they went to work making the manse livable. Loucile continues in her letter:

> We "fixed" two rooms and managed to exist until the Wakefield Church came to our aid with the greatest and most pleasant surprise of our new career with which we bought comfortable furniture for the living room, one bedroom, and the kitchen. Later, thru [*sic*] a grant from the National Board and labor contributed by men of the community, we plastered the kitchen and built a new back porch. We painted the floors and woodwork and papered two of the down stairs rooms . . . We are quiet [*sic*] proud of what we have accomplished with small expense and much hard work.

The Board of National Missions had taken them up on Gene's offer to work for a minimum salary. Their salary started at $90 per month and was soon dropped to $60 per month. Over the next several years, they would refurbish another manse at Big Lick and eventually add a room onto it. The two manses they inherited were drafty, uninsulated, barn-like structures. Providing comfortable living space for their family would remain a constant chore. Their living arrangements were comparable to or better than those of the people among whom they ministered, and that was what mattered more to them. Gene Smathers complained occasionally about his small salary—not that it was too small, but that it was too large, thereby giving him a cash income greater than the majority of the folk among whom he ministered and potentially establishing a barrier between him and them.

What Smathers had *not* bargained for was that three of the four churches were in various stages of failure. From 1870–1920, northern missionaries swarmed to Southern Appalachia like grasshoppers to a hay field. The American Missionary Association and most northern "mainline" Protestant churches switched their focus from overseas (primarily Africa) to Southern Appalachia. Within the South, they shifted from ministry to African American Freedmen (especially through the establishment of Freedmen's schools) to the establishment of schools and churches for "Southern Mountain Whites." This was the denominations' term for the people residing in the mountainous regions of seven Southern states—West Virginia, Kentucky, Virginia, North Carolina, Tennessee, Georgia, and Alabama. It was not a term the mountain folk applied to themselves, nor did they take kindly to it, considering its use by outsiders to be the equivalent of "poor white trash."[1]

Henry D. Shapiro in *Appalachia on Our Mind*, in his chapter on "Protestant Home Missions," says that the missionaries came to the "Mountain South" because of the perceived "peculiarities" of the people and the perception that the "otherness" of Appalachian life and culture were so foreign to the American mainstream that the people were "in but not of America."[2] Southern Appalachia was seen as "unchurched" by these denominations because their denominations were not represented there. They came in droves because in their view, the Mountain South needed to be Christianized and Americanized.[3] They proceeded in apparent ignorance of the fact that there were already many independent churches throughout the region, and people from the region had won a decisive battle in the Revolutionary War at Kings Mountain and many had fought valiantly for the Union during the civil war.

Because of the relative isolation of the mountaineers from the rest of the South that "preserved" them from the taint of slavery and prevented their full complicity with the "slavocracy," [sic] it was assumed that they were both more "deserving of and more amenable to the ministrations of the northern agencies of benevolence."[4] Shapiro, like the missionaries before him, fails to note that much of the mountain South remained loyal to the Union during the civil war, including the state of West Virginia, most of East Tennessee, and as far south as Georgia and Alabama. Over 100,000 Union troops came from the Southern Mountain states.

Shapiro states that "preaching stations and churches, day schools, boarding schools, academies and normal schools were established as convenience dictated, and tended for obvious reasons to cluster around the larger centers of populations."[5] This may help to explain the Presbyterian Church at Grassy Cove but does not really explain how or why the Presbyterian Church got to the other three locations.

For Ozone and Jewett, the Presbyterian presence is better explained by David Whisnant, in the opening paragraph of his book *Modernizing the Mountaineer*, where he writes,

> The opening of the Appalachian region to large-scale economic exploitation during the last third of the nineteenth century coincided, as the opening of new colonies frequently does, with the coming of hundreds of missionaries. The first trains to reach many an Appalachian county seat bore not only the advance agents and engineers employed by the coal barons . . . but also the preachers and missionary ladies sent by the denominations to harvest the bountiful crop of unchurched souls reputed to have burrowed back into the hollows, and to teach the swarms of children thought to be growing up in heathen illiteracy. By the turn of the century . . . there were scores of new churches and 'church and independent schools' scattered throughout the region.[6]

This is not an entirely accurate statement as it ignores other relevant factors and is about all Whisnant has to say about the denominational venture into Appalachia between 1870 and 1920. However, it contains more than a grain of truth in explaining why some of the missionaries came, to whom they were beholden, and why they failed.

As limited as this analysis may be, it is foolhardy to ignore the role of northern capitalists, speculators, industrialists, and entrepreneurs who came by the trainload to acquire the rights to the timber, coal, and other minerals that grew on or lay beneath the Appalachian hills. They often used tricky deeds and con-man tactics, and in many cases, they were members of the denominations and provided much of the money that funded the missionary adventure. It was in their interest to have more stable, sedate, and controllable churches than the fiercely independent and emotionally fervent native churches in the region. This exposed the churches to the same boom-and-bust cycle as occurred in the camps and communities established by the coal and timber barons.

No matter how astute and/or correct Shapiro's and Whisnant's more contemporary analyses may be, still the best explanation of why Smathers's churches and hundreds of others like them were failing was presented in a much older study of the Southern Mountains (the research was completed prior to 1921). In John C. Campbell's *The Southern Highlander & his Homeland*, in his chapter on the "Religious Life of the Rural Highlands," he sets forth three reasons for the missionaries' failure. First, he says, was "a too general tendency prevails on the part of both pastors and teachers to force upon the mountain people modes and methods natural in other regions but unnatural to the mountaineer." [7] A second reason, he says, is the expectations of "results" (converts) too quickly so that pastors were frequently not left on the field long enough to produce results.[8]

The third reason may have best been expressed by an old mountaineer ("the father of one of the most noted feud leaders") quoted by Campbell. "'You are wondering,' said he to Campbell, 'why the missionaries among the Highlanders are a failure. I will tell you. Their missionaries are failures because the men the church sends were failures before they came. They have sent to us ministers who have no brains or gumption—ministers who could not get a church anywhere else. If you are to touch the hearts of these Highlanders you must send us the bravest men, the most able and consecrated women you can find, Give us the men and women who can make a success in any place, and they will make a success here.'"[9]

The one exception to the paradigms set forth by Shapiro, Whisnant, and Campbell was the church at Big Lick. The Big Lick community consisted of about fifty families (three hundred individuals) spread out over 12.5 square miles of territory—about the same area as Grassy Cove. Whereas the Cove was home to several prominent businessmen and influential citizens, Big Lick was not. The Cove was a Presbyterian kind of place. Big Lick was not. Big Lick was situated on a wild edge of the county and had no prominent business or professional men and few, if any, influential citizens.

Big Lick was not anything like the Cove. It had maybe three hundred acres of cropland versus the three thousand in the Cove. Moreover, unlike the Cove, the Big Lick soil was not good cropland. It was acidic and deficient in phosphate. There were no prosperous farmers there. Most people had enough land for a garden and maybe a milk cow, but no more than six of the homesteads could be called farms. Even these were small—no more than two hundred acres with no more than fifty acres of that in cultivation. The average household income was less than $50 per year.

Unlike Jewett and Ozone, in 1917, when the Presbyterian work began there, Big Lick had no extractable minerals (later in the 1950s, some building stone would be quarried). There was, in 1917, no expectation of a population boom related to mineral wealth. Moreover, by 1910, all the virgin timber was gone, and the second-growth forests were of poor quality exacerbated by the practice of burning them off every spring so grasses and seedlings would grow up to provide grazing for open-range cattle and hogs. Most of the cattle and hogs that ran wild in the woods were brought in by larger farmers from the neighboring Sequatchie Valley.

Moreover, it was isolated—three miles from the nearest state-maintained road with dirt roads that were often impassable in the winter. It was at the very southern edge of Cumberland County and bounded by creeks, ridges, and bluffs on two sides and large absentee-owned tracts of land on the other two sides, which the owners would not sell in small tracts (the size tracts needed to be affordable to Big Lick farmers). This allowed no room for growth. Nevertheless, the community had a school, though they sometimes had trouble getting a teacher.

The plurality of the population was Methodist, including a retired Methodist circuit-riding preacher. The remainder were either Baptists or had no religious affiliation. Churches had come and gone, but in 1917, there was no functioning church in the community.

There was nothing to recommend it, and it was so isolated that it probably would have gone unnoticed by the Presbyterian leaders and bureaucrats in New York, Lebanon, and Sparta, Tennessee—except for the action of the community itself. In 1916, the community selected its most capable leader and sent him as an emissary to the local presbytery. His mission was to plead with the presbytery to send a community worker to Big Lick. They did not ask for a pastor; they did not ask for a church. They simply wanted someone working regularly for the cause of Christ in their community, and they were more than willing to accept a woman and a Presbyterian.

In 1917, the Presbyterian Church responded by sending Mrs. Carrie Murphy, a former schoolteacher from Chattanooga, as a community worker.[10] A woman of great wisdom, compassion, and perseverance, Mrs. Murphy stayed in the community for seventeen years until she retired in 1934. Under her leadership, the community organized a Ladies Aid Society, built a new two-room school building, sent several of its young people away to boarding high schools where they could get their teaching certificate, and in 1921 organized a Presbyterian church. A woman who was willing to push boundaries, Murphy did everything that an organizing pastor would do although at the time, the Presbyterian Church did not ordain women. The ordination of women as pastors would wait another twenty-five years.

Though it was the youngest of his four churches, within the first three months of his time on the field, Smathers chose Big Lick as the place he eventually wanted to be. In his first quarterly report from the field, he wrote of Big Lick:

> Due to the excellent work of Mrs. Murphy the Big Lick church is in the best condition of the four, and I believe we will be able to develop and carry out a rather comprehensive program [there].

Big Lick was the only one of the churches that prospered during Gene Smathers's thirty-six years in the county, and it did so only after the split of the parish in 1934. It did so partially because of the nature of the community itself, partially because of the foundation laid by Mrs. Murphy and partially by the Grace of God because it was burdened with none of the reasons for failure outlined by Shapiro, Whisnant, and Campbell. Especially important was the quality and perseverance of the leadership sent to the Big Lick church. In Murphy and Smathers, Big Lick was blessed with two of the most capable, energetic, and visionary persons in their entire denomination. Since both spent their entire careers there, the Big Lick Church had only one change in leadership in fifty-three years.

NOTES

1. Michael Smathers, personal knowledge from growing up in the Appalachian South, from his teaching of Appalachian Studies for several years, and from his own personal research. The people referred to themselves as "highlanders," "mountain people," or "hill folks."
2. Henry D. Shapiro, *Appalachia on Our Mind*, University of North Carolina Press, 1978, pp. 32–58.
3. Ibid, Shapiro 41–43.
4. Ibid, Shapiro 39.
5. Ibid, Shapiro 53.
6. David E. Whisnant, *Modernizing the Mountaineer* (New York: Burt Franklin & Company, 1980), 3.
7. John C. Campbell, *The Southern Highlander & His Homeland*, copyrighted and published posthumously first by the Russell Sage Foundation in 1921 and then recopyrighted and published again in 1969 by the University Press of Kentucky, p. 190. Ibid, Campbell 191.
8. Ibid, Campbell 192.
9. "Community workers" were single women, often widows, who were placed in communities that the Presbyterian Board of National Missions had selected as service points, but where they were unable to place a full-time minister. Sometimes the communities had an established church, but often they did not. The community workers did various types of work, including teaching and sometimes preaching.

CHAPTER 4

"WE MADE IT WITH OUR OWN HANDS"

January 22, 1934, to May 30, 1935

MONDAY, JANUARY 22, 1934, CROSSVILLE, TENNESSEE: Three hundred hungry men fanned out today across a 10,000-acre tract of land once owned by the Missouri Coal and Land Company four miles south of here. They are the first cadre of men who will build the Cumberland Homestead, a 250-family planned community developed under the auspices of the Division of Subsistence Homesteads, U.S. Department of the Interior. Popularized by Ralph Borsodi's book *Flight from the City*, the concept of subsistence homesteading gained official sanction as section 208 of Title II of the New Deal's National Industrial Recovery Act of 1933.

The Cumberland Homestead is the nineteenth of these planned communities. The planners envision a utopian society in which stranded industrial workers, out-of-work miners and mill hands, and starving farmers will come together to create a cooperative community in which they will live together, work together, play together, and worship together, though worship is the least of their concerns. They envisioned a single community church. Very quickly, they were surrounded by a Methodist, a Baptist, and a Cambellite church. Their community church never made it out of the ground.[1]

Later that same morning, a small family packed up their old Model A Ford with their few worldly belongings and moved across Cumberland County from Ozone to Big Lick. They too have a utopian vision. Though less grandiose, their vision is no less ambitious, no less compelling, and no less challenging than that of the government planners. It is the vision of a Christian rural community—a community with the church and worship of God at its very core, but one in which that church and its worship would reach out to shape every aspect of life in the community. It would be a community of Christian brothers and sisters that reached out in love not only to each other but to all others, including specifically persons of other races, nationalities, and creeds. That family's name was Smathers—Eugene, Loucile, and their infant daughter, Pat. Unknown to the family at that time, this would be the last move they would ever make. Of this move, Gene Smathers later wrote,

> I had come to remain as long as I could be of effective service in building a Christian rural community. The details of this community were not clear . . . but I felt that they would appear as we sought to solve our problems. However there were two definite objectives: the building of a church which would be a House of Worship and a center for the various community activities; [and] the development of a recreation program for the youth.[2]

The Smatherses had first set foot in Big Lick eighteen months earlier when Gene became the missionary pastor of the Cumberland County Presbyterian Parish with churches at Ozone, Grassy Cove, Jewett, and Big Lick. Big Lick was the youngest of the churches and in some ways the most isolated of the communities. The Smatherses were replacing an exceptional church professional who had lived and worked with the people of Big Lick for seventeen years.

Spoken of above, her name was Carrie Murphy. She was one of the community workers who served under the auspices of the Presbyterian Board of National Missions. She had come to Big Lick at the specific invitation of the community. So great was their respect for her that she was ordained an elder in the Big Lick Church in 1933, two decades before the denomination officially sanctioned the ordination of women as elders. A church ahead of its time.

Within three months of their first arrival in Big Lick in 1932, the Smatherses noted several factors that caused them to think that Big Lick would present the most promising field of their four churches. Among those factors were the following: the groundwork laid by Mrs. Murphy; exceptional senior leadership that was open to new ideas and new ways of doing things; a strong tradition of neighbors helping neighbors; a large number of young people; and only one church.

At age seventy, Murphy had stayed five years past the usual retirement age in the hope that the church would find someone to replace her. Church officials considered closing the work at Big Lick when she retired, which was scheduled for December 31, 1933. Gene Smathers persuaded them to split the parish, continue the work at Big Lick, and permit him to move there as a resident pastor after Mrs. Murphy retired. He would continue as pastor at Jewett, as well as Big Lick. Grassy Cove was closed. Ozone was continued but dropped from his parish. During his thirty-six years of ministry at Big Lick, Smathers continued also to serve the church at Jewett.

SUNDAY, JANUARY 28, 1934, BIG LICK SCHOOLHOUSE: After church service today, Gene Smathers introduced to the church elders and deacons the idea of building a church. It was one of two clear objectives he had in mind when he moved to Big Lick. (The other was establishing a recreation program for the youth.) However, such a thing appeared to be a remote dream. As one of them told the young pastor, "Preacher, we can't hardly afford church as it is. How can we build a new church building?" The young preacher knew that a real church building was key to implementing his vision of a Christian rural community. However, he also knew how little income the people had; after all, they could only pay him in produce from their gardens and farms. The dream of a new church building seemed distant at best.

WEDNESDAY, FEBRUARY 7, 1934, THE PRESBYTERIAN MANSE, BIG LICK, TENNESSEE: The Session and Deacons of the Big Lick Presbyterian Church met today and established a building fund. The fund is to receive proceeds from birthday offerings, the Lord's Hen Club, and the Lord's Acre Club. In these latter two organizations, women set aside a small amount of their egg money and men a small amount of their crop income for the church. *They also voted to establish a recreation program for young people.* (emphasis added)

TUESDAY, APRIL 3, 1934, PRESBYTERY MEETING, FIRST PRESBYTERIAN CHURCH, SPARTA, TENNESSEE: The Reverend Eugene Smathers learned today of someone who might help with the building of a church at Big Lick. The word came from the Reverend Charles T. Greenway, southeastern field representative of the Board of National Mission. Rev. Greenway reported that the Reverend Dr. Warren H. Wilson, superintendent, Department of Church and Country Life of the Board of National Missions, knew a Presbyterian elder in Cincinnati, Ohio, who might be able and willing to help finance the construction of a church somewhere within the bounds of the Cumberland Mountain Presbytery. No promises were made to Big Lick.

The Reverend Dr. Warren H. Wilson, who at age sixty-seven was near the end of a long and distinguished career in the rural church field, had taken a liking to Smathers a few years earlier. Smathers, in turn, had been greatly influenced by Wilson and his writings. He had come to accept Wilson's contention that the church is a "social as well as a divine institution." Like Wilson, he saw the rural church as an engine for the improvement of life for rural folk and their communities. For many years after completion of the Big Lick Church building, a picture of Dr. Warren H. Wilson was prominently displayed in the church.

The elder who was to become Big Lick's patron was James Wilson Brown. Mr. Brown was a personal secretary to William C. Proctor, president of Procter & Gamble. Though not a wealthy man himself, Mr. Brown continued to have a steady salary even in the midst of the Depression. He had also invested prudently and was known for his generosity. He loved the Cumberland Plateau and had become a friend to its people through his many hunting trips there. He had not been to Big Lick (it was too isolated), but he had often stayed at Crab Orchard, which was in the vicinity. It was not known at this time how much Mr. Brown might be willing to give, nor exactly where nor how he might want his gift to be used.

MONDAY, APRIL 23, 1934, THE PRESBYTERIAN MANSE, BIG LICK, TENNESSEE: The Big Lick Session and Deacons met today to discuss plans for a church building. Rev. Smathers has had further correspondence with the Board of National Missions regarding the possibility that Mr. James Wilson Brown of Cincinnati might be willing to help finance the construction of a church at Big Lick. It appears that there is a real possibility that this could happen. Plans for a new building were discussed, and the men present were appointed as a building committee. The members of that committee are Thomas L. "Uncle Tom" Hale; Albert H. Hall; W. Vance Burgess; T. Virgil Hale; J. Harrison Tollett; and Estille Burgess. Plans were made to work up cost estimates for a new building and to canvas the community for pledges of labor and materials.

FRIDAY, JUNE 15, 1934, BIG LICK, TENNESSEE: James Wilson Brown ended a tour of mission projects on the Cumberland Plateau today with a stop in Big Lick. He was impressed with the work there and expressed interest in their desire for a church building. He and the Reverend Eugene Smathers, pastor of the Big Lick parish, liked each other although it was an odd coupling from the get-go. On the one hand, there was Brown, a middle aged well-to-do capitalist, a dyed-in-the-wool conservative Republican who disliked FDR and hated the New Deal. On the other hand was Smathers, a young preacher radicalized by a summer in a Kentucky coal camp, a radical Roosevelt Democrat who had even dabbled a bit with socialism. Though it would appear that their friendship should be doomed, it would grow and prosper over the years to come.

THURSDAY, JULY 5, 1934, THE MANSE, BIG LICK, TENNESSEE: Gene Smathers received a copy of a letter James Wilson Brown had sent to the Reverend Paul E. Doran expressing his interest in the Big Lick parish and setting forth two conditions Big Lick had to meet before he would consent to making a contribution toward the building of a church. Brown had sent the letter to Doran because Doran was the senior National Missions pastor on the Cumberland Plateau and superintendent of the presbytery of Cumberland Mountain. He had not sent a copy of the letter to Smathers and neither had Doran. It is not known why neither man sent a copy of the letter to Smathers. However, Smathers thought that Doran deliberately kept the information from Smathers so that Big Lick would miss Brown's deadline and Doran could use the money for a project of his own. Such was the politics of the church even among small churches in a small presbytery.

Smathers got his copy from someone else at the Board of National Missions, most likely Dr. Warren H. Wilson or the Reverend Charles T. Greenway. The conditions Brown placed on his contribution was that Big Lick have an experienced mason to lay the stonework for the building and that the parish secure sufficient acreage for a church farm. Big Lick had until the end of August to meet these conditions. Dr. Wilson seemed confident that he could help Big Lick locate a suitable mason.

However, the need to secure land for a church farm would have to be solved locally. Mrs. Carrie Murphy owned the twenty-three acres on which the church was to be located. She had agreed to give the church one acre for the building. They now needed her whole twenty-three-acre tract.

Gene Smathers desperately needed to communicate with Mrs. Murphy. However, they were, at this time, about as isolated from each other as two people could be and still be in the United States. Smathers was in Big Lick, an isolated mail outpost, and Murphy was visiting Indian villages in the sagebrush country along the Snake and Salmon Rivers in Idaho. Both places still received some or all of their mail by horseback.

SATURDAY, JULY 14, 1934, BIG LICK, TENNESSEE In a letter today, Gene Smathers wrote to Carrie Murphy:

> I would have written you before concerning the work here but have not known your address since you have been traveling... I suppose some of the folk have told you in their letters about our plans for a new church building. We have at last begun to see our dream come true. At the present time we have an offer from Mr. Brown of Cincinnati, and if we can meet the conditions by the last of Aug. we will actually be able to begin our building...
>
> For some reason, Mr. Doran has seen fit to keep us in the dark concerning Mr. Brown's proposals. Mr. Brown visited Big Lick and was much interested. But instead of sending us his proposals, he sent them to Mr. Doran, and it is only indirectly that we became aware of the conditions which we have to meet...
>
> Without realizing it you are in a position which will largely decide whether or not we are able to meet the conditions set by Mr. Brown... I am anxious, therefore, to know what you would take for your land, if you would sell at all...
>
> We had hoped you would give us a plot for the church on the knoll just above the house here. We knew that you had

said you would do this whenever we could build a church. But the introduction of the whole plot into Mr. Brown's conditions places the whole matter for the time being in your hands.

SATURDAY, JULY 21, 1934, MELBA, IDAHO: In reply to Smathers's letter, Carrie Murphy wrote,

> Your letter came while I was away on a little visit with a friend out in the sage brush on the Snake River . . . I am writing as early as I can hoping I will be in time . . .
>
> I had thought to keep that land for a summer home possibly, but I will gladly sell it to have a church at Big Lick . . .
>
> I will sell the 23 acres for the cost, interest on the years I have held it, and taxes paid. I have estimated it and it is $350.00.

MONDAY–TUESDAY, JULY 30–31, 1934, THE MANSE, BIG LICK, TENNESSEE: The Session and Deacons held a two-day meeting as the building committee and took the following actions:

- Elected Eugene Smathers as secretary
- Reviewed the proposed plans prepared by Architect A. M. Ballantyne of New York
- Adopted a cost estimate of $4,000 for the building
- Approved the site for the building
- Voted to purchase the twenty-three acres from Mrs. Carrie Murphy for $350

TUESDAY, SEPTEMBER 18, 1934, BIG LICK, TENNESSEE: In meetings over the last three days, Smathers and the Reverend Greenway worked out the final plans for the church. As originally prepared by Mr. Ballantyne, the plans were for a sanctuary only. Smathers insisted that the building include a social hall for community meetings and recreation, a kitchen, and Sunday school rooms. (Note to twenty-first-century readers: Today it would be called a "family life center," and many churches have one. In 1934, it was a radical idea that was roundly condemned by other preachers in the area. Like in many things, the Big Lick church was ahead of the times.)

TUESDAY, SEPTEMBER 19, 1934, BIG LICK, TENNESSEE: In a letter to Gene's mother written last night, Loucile Smathers wrote,

> Gene & some of the men are working on the church. They cleared the ground off yesterday and carried stone . . . We had a man here from the board for a few days & he & Gene worked out the plans for the building. The church part will be of stone and the parish house, which will have a large social room, kitchen, and class rooms will be made of wood. It's really two buildings but looks like one from the front. They will be connected with a stone porch of a thing. The church will have a stone floor made of this native stone. Gene will draw a plan of it on the back of this letter so you can kinda [sic] tell how it will be . . . We'll know for sure in a few days now about the money part. The labor is most all donated. It will be a $4000 building.

The sketch that Gene Smathers drew on this letter is shown at the end of this chapter. As finally built, the building did not look exactly like this drawing. It ended up being a single building with two wings, but it did include a social room, a kitchen/Sunday school room, a Sunday school room/library, an alcove for another Sunday school room and overflow space, and a bell tower with a cross on top. There existed such misunderstanding of the place for a cross that many in the area thought the church was Roman Catholic.

MONDAY, SEPTEMBER 24, 1934, THE MANSE, BIG LICK, TENNESSEE: The Session and Deacons met as the building committee today and were told that the Board of National Missions had received the gift from Mr. James W. Brown. They requested that the committee secretary write Mrs. Murphy for the deed to the land.

TUESDAY, SEPTEMBER 25, 1934, BIG LICK, TENNESSEE: Gene Smathers wrote to Carrie Murphy in Melba, Idaho today:

> I am sure you will be pleased to know that we are going forward with our new church building . . . It is our plans now to be able to begin the stone work in about three weeks . . . I am sending some orders for materials this A.M.
>
> At the meeting of the building committee yesterday, I was authorized as secretary to inform you that the $350.00 is available for you just as soon as you can give us a deed to the land . . . The committee feels the sooner we close the deal with you the better it will be for all concerned.

MONDAY, OCTOBER 8, 1934, 611 ELINOR STREET, CHATTANOOGA, TENNESSEE: Carrie Murphy wrote to Gene Smathers today:

> Your letter was forwarded to me from Idaho. I am ready at any time to make a deed to that land . . .
>
> Mr. Hale, Uncle Tom, drew [my] deed and I can send it to you and you can have [a new one] made and recorded. If this gives assurance to them who need assuring, it can be done at once.

TUESDAY, OCTOBER 23, 1934, BIG LICK, TENNESSEE: The Session and Deacons met as the building committee today to discuss a contact with Mr. Charles L. Mitchell to do the stonework on the church. Mr. Mitchell has just finished with the stonework on several buildings at Asheville Farm School in Swannanoa, North Carolina (a National Missions school that in 1942 would become Warren H. Wilson College). "After some discussion, the Committee voted to give

Mr. Mitchell the contract." Plans were made by which the community could fulfill its part of the contract. It was decided that Deacon Harrison Tollett would serve as carpenter. Only one rock in the building will not come from Big Lick. Mr. Mitchell will bring it with him from North Carolina.

MONDAY, OCTOBER 29, 1934, THE KNOLL ABOVE THE MANSE, BIG LICK, TENNESSEE: Work began in earnest today on the new church building. The men of the community began digging the ditches and filling them with rock crushed by sledgehammers, which will serve as the foundation for the stone walls that are scheduled to get started next week.

SUNDAY, NOVEMBER 4, 1934, THE SCHOOLHOUSE, BIG LICK, TENNESSEE: The Session and Deacons met after church today.

> Motion was made that a bronze tablet in honor of Mr. James W. Brown be secured by donations from the community and placed over the fireplace in social room of the new building. Estille Burgess was appointed to collect this fund.

TUESDAY, NOVEMBER 6, 1934, BIG LICK, TENNESSEE: Mr. Charles L. Mitchell from North Carolina arrived in Big Lick yesterday. He is presently staying with Estille and Dora Burgess. They are newlyweds with no children. They have room for him and are glad to provide his room and board for a few weeks. Mr. Mitchell will board with different families in the community while he is here to work on the new church building. That is part of the community's contract with him.

TUESDAY, DECEMBER 25, CHRISTMAS DAY, 1934, BIG LICK, TENNESSEE: Things are kind of quiet around here this week as work on the new church building is at a standstill. Mr. Mitchell has gone home for the holidays and will return next week. The weather has been good, and the stonework on the building is progressing nicely. The two chimneys are complete. The chimney for the social room sits out all by itself thirty feet from any other part of the building. Folks around here think it is the strangest thing they ever saw, two chimneys built before the building with nothing to support them. They wonder how they will ever stand up.

At the Smatherses' house over the holidays, time was spent studying the blueprints for the church building. No one in Big Lick has ever seen a real set of blueprints drawn by an architect before. The only one that really understands them is Mr. Mitchell. When he has finished the stonework and is gone, the folks will be on their own as far as reading the blueprints is concerned. The only other person that has ever seen anything like a blueprint is Loucile Smathers. Her mother's family were millwrights and she had worked in a hardware store, so she had seen some rough drawings of mills and such before she was married.

Pastor Smathers is serving as foreman of the project and has been burning the midnight oil under a kerosene lamp studying the blueprints. He has to study the blueprints every night so that he can direct the work the following day. He now thinks he can figure them out with the help of Harrison Tollett and Estille Burgess who have the most building experience among the men working on the building. When the church building began, his wife said, he was barely able to use a hammer and saw, but now he is a skilled construction foreman.

SUNDAY, MARCH 24, 1935, THE SCHOOLHOUSE, BIG LICK, TENNESSEE: The Session and Deacons met after church today and among other things began to make plans for the dedication of the new church building. The work is progressing nicely. Practically all the stonework is complete, including the stone floor in the church. The men laid that themselves with a little help from Mr. Mitchell. They had never worked with stone before, but they got it pretty level and are plenty proud of that floor.

All that is left of the stonework is a little on the high gable ends of the building. Elmo Bradley and Eucle Burgess have been competing to see who can hoist the biggest rock up a ladder to put in place at the top of the gables. The big stone that Mr. Mitchell brought from North Carolina was put in place last week. It occupies a prominent place right in the middle of the front gable above the big window.

SUNDAY, APRIL 21, 1935, THE SCHOOLHOUSE, BIG LICK, TENNESSEE: At a meeting of the congregation of the Big Lick Presbyterian Church held today, the congregation overwhelmingly selected the name Calvary for the new building. The minutes from that meeting record that three names—Bethany, Trinity, and Calvary—were nominated, and

> the name Calvary received a large majority of the vote. And motion was made and carried that the Presbytery of Cumberland Mountain be petitioned to the effect that henceforth the church here be known as Calvary Church of Big Lick, Presbyterian.

May 30th was set as the day of dedication.

FRIDAY, MAY 10, NEW CHURCH SITE, BIG LICK, TENNESSEE: The building is nearing completion. The windows are all in. All that remains is the board and batten siding for the social room, some interior work, finishing the pews, pulpit and communion table, and installing the bell. They were $70 short of the $220 needed for the bell, but Dr. Warren H. Wilson personally made an extra gift that enabled them to purchase the bell.

Teenagers Elmo Bradley and Eucle Burgess put the finishing touches on the stone wall above the front door the other day. They found a dead mole and covered it with concrete on top of that wall. They shaped the concrete like a turtle with its head peeking over the wall. "That way," they said, "we'll always have something looking over us when we go to church."

THURSDAY, MAY 30, 1935, CALVARY CHURCH, BIG LICK, TENNESSEE: An estimated four hundred people gathered today for the dedication of Calvary Church of Big Lick, Presbyterian. The dedication address was delivered by the Reverend Dr. E. Graham Wilson, general secretary, Board of National Missions, Presbyterian Church, USA. The service lasted three hours with dinner on the grounds afterward.

The building is a beautiful stone and wood structure. Designed to resemble an old English country church, it has a stone exterior with a dark wood interior. The attached social hall is built of wood around a stone fireplace. The church was constructed over six months in the dead of winter with at least one person working on each of 147 days during that time. When they began in November, 1934, they had hoped to finish the building in time for spring planting.

Certain items were placed in a glass canning jar and sealed inside the cornerstone. Among the items placed in that jar was a list of those who had contributed labor on the building. This list revealed that a total of 42 men gave over 475 man-days of labor plus fifty-one-plus days of a man with a team. This labor was valued at $948.00. Another list revealed that they had received $3,514.50 in cash contributions. Of that amount, $3,192.00 was given by James Wilson Brown of Cincinnati, Ohio. In a verbal report, Pastor Smathers reported that they spent $3,514.30 and had $0.20 left over when they finished. Thus, it can be said that they brought the project in on time and under budget.[3, 4]

One of the elders said, "This church is ours. We built it ourselves. We put up the beams, we made the pulpit and the communion table, we made the pews, we laid the stone floor. Some of us had never worked with concrete before, but we learned how, and we did it. We made it with our own hands."

"Calvary Church under construction – 1935."

"Calvary Church under construction – 1935."

"Calvary Church, 1940, as it looked new."

NOTES

1. Mike Smathers, "The Search for the Garden," *Southern Exposure* 8, no. 1 (Spring 1980): 57–63.
2. Smathers, op. cit., *"I Work In the Cumberlands,"* pamphlet published by the Fellowship of Southern Churchmen in 1940. Also published in *Rural America*, The American Country Life Association Inc., 18, no. 7 (October 1940): 3–7.
3. The remainder of the material comes from the church's official session (board) minutes book and from Eugene Smathers's journals and correspondence.
4. An article on the building and planned dedication of the church also is recorded in the *Crossville Chronicle*, published on Thursday, May 23, 1935.

CHAPTER 5

"AN OUNCE OF PREVENTION ... A POUND OF CURE"

You see things as they are; and you ask, "Why?"
But I dream things that never were: and I ask, "why not?"

—George Bernard Shaw

THE HEALTH CENTER, BIG LICK, TENNESSEE, JUNE 22, 1938: Dignitaries from around the county and at least four other states gathered in Big Lick today to dedicate the Warren H. Wilson House of Health, known throughout the community simply as "the Health Center." It will provide preventive and acute care to all families in the community through an inexpensive subscription plan. The facility is named for Dr. Warren H. Wilson who was instrumental in helping the community get support and financing for the building. However, the vision for the building came from the young pastor, Eugene Smathers.

He had moved to the community in 1934 with two "definite objectives": building a church and starting a recreation program for the youth. By 1936, both of these objectives had been realized. Of the latter activity, Smathers had written:

> [At first] we made a feeble beginning with a recreational program. There was much prejudice and opposition to overcome. But we moved slowly . . . We have depended chiefly upon folk games and dances for many hours of joyous and wholesome fun . . . I feel that [this program] has been one of our best contributions not only to the community but to the whole region. Our "socials" are both famous and infamous . . . Our severest critics . . . bemoan the fact that the youth are going to "hell" via the road-house. One who has not tried to promote some sort of recreational program in a similar situation in the mountains cannot fully appreciate the sense of achievement which is ours . . . Seeking to bring joy and gaiety into drab and dull surroundings will always be an important element in our program.[1]

Some of Smathers's friends felt that it was time for the Smatherses to move on to another parish. On December 28, 1936, Gene Smathers wrote in his journal:

> The Drakes [seminary and lifelong friends] came about noon . . . Enjoyed their visit. Louis somewhat discouraged, Mary Henri wanting to move again. They tried to advise me that a change would be good for me—But I continue to believe that I have work to do here as long as the folk want me & will respond to my leadership. I want to help establish a Health Center, for I know the need.

Smathers would later write,

> One of the most pressing problems is that of health and medical care. Due to poor housing, lack in quality if not in quantity of food, and other causes, there has been an unusual amount of sickness . . . and the cost of medical care is prohibitive. [For families whose cash incomes average less than $50.00 per year], one visit from the doctor costs from $10.00 to $15.00 and must be paid in cash or secured by a

mortgage. I have known families who had to sell their only cow to pay a doctor bill or even mortgage their little bit of land. This cost leads a family to wait until it is too late for medical care to do any good and yet the members have to struggle for months to pay the bill . . . [Thus] our next major undertaking [after building of the church and the youth recreation program] was the development of a health program . . . I have mentioned the prohibitive cost of medical care. But the actual situation could not be described—it had to be experienced.[2]

Nevertheless, in a paper entitled "Health in the Big Lick Community" written in 1937, Smathers had made an effort to describe the situation, writing,

> Approximately 75% of the school children have some physical defect or weakness which could be remedied or cured by adequate medical and dental care...
>
> Cumberland County has only six doctors, all located at some distance from [Big Lick and nearby communities]. The cost of one visit from a doctor is from $10 to $20. The charge at child-birth is $40. And money must be on hand or [the doctor] will not come at any price . . . One of the chief services of the pastor and his car has been to take sick folk to the doctor. There are months when no doctor visits any of these neighborhoods.

The Smatherses had experienced their own troubles with inadequate health care. Their son, Charles, was born on May 15, 1935, with a congenital heart defect. He suffered from the blue baby syndrome, a symptomatic diagnosis that can be caused from a number of conditions, some of them rather mild and some of them life-threatening. Given the state of medical science in those days, Charles might not have lived even if he had experienced better care.

When he got pneumonia, the Smatherses took him to the nearest hospital, a small rudimentary facility in Rockwood, Tennessee. The doctors and nurses there did the best they could for him and utilized the most effective treatments they had; but on March 19, 1936, Charles Boydston Smathers, ten months old, took his last breath and died.

On December 31, 1936, Gene Smathers wrote in his journal: "1936 soon will be gone. 1937? I wonder what it holds? Live today! 1936 has on the whole been happy! Lost Baby Charles, a loss and a gain: Loss of a precious little life, a gain in understanding of life's tragedies & sorrows. My first immediate experience with death. I feel that I must make his contribution to life, as well as our own. The loss bound us together as no other experience." The loss also reinforced his dream of a health center for Big Lick.

On January 1, 1937, he wrote in his journal:

> 1937 is here . . . Had letter from Dr. Warren H. Wilson concerning health center & a possibility of getting it, if the funds for the support of a nurse can be secured. He wanted me to suggest possible sources—I wish I knew of some. This is more difficult than securing money for the building . . . I trust that we will succeed—no greater service can be rendered with so small relative cost. It was an encouraging letter for New Year's Day, however, & I have faith to believe that Jan. 1, 1938, will see another dream realized. Life is a series of expectations!

Three months later, Warren Wilson was dead. Gene Smathers wrote in his journal: "A great rural leader is gone." Wilson had been the principal advocate for the Board of National Missions to allocate funds for a clinic at Big Lick. His death, therefore, caused Gene Smathers some concern, but it did not cause him to pause in his own advocacy for the clinic. By May 1937, he convinced the board along with Big Lick's chief benefactor, James Wilson Brown of Cincinnati, to back the effort.

The Reverend Charles Greenway had replaced Dr. Wilson at the Board of National Missions. On May 12, 1937, Gene Smathers wrote in his journal: "Had note from Mr. Greenway today saying he was bringing good news & this week's copy of Monday Morning [a magazine for Presbyterian clergy] let the cat out of the bag by stating in an article concerning the meeting of the Board of National Missions, that a health center had been approved for Big Lick. Another dream near realization—but the realization means another period of strenuous effort."

On May 13, 1937, his journal includes this notation: "When I got home, Mr. Greenway was here. We had a nice visit and discussed the health center. We have $3,000.00 for a building [from James Wilson Brown] & the Board has made a grant of $1,500.00 per year for maintenance. This is a new venture & offers real opportunity for constructive work, also the possibility for abject failure. I am almost totally ignorant of such health centers and their work."

In fact, the venture was in many ways a shot in the dark. The proposed idea was cutting-edge even by twenty-first-century standards. In 1937, it was largely unheard of—at least in the rural South. It was to be a subscription health service and medical cooperative that was premised on preventive care. Families would pay a modest annual fee, and in turn, all their preventive health services would be provided by a resident nurse.

There would be two clinics per month with an attending physician. One of these, the "Well Baby Clinic," was free to expectant mothers and mothers with pre-school-age children. In order to have the nurse in attendance at childbirth, expectant mothers had to attend these clinics. For acute and emergency care and for the "General Clinic" patients would pay a minuscule fee-for-service ranging from ten to twenty-five cents ($0.10– $0.25).

The fees thus generated had to cover the cost of a resident nurse and the twice-a-month doctors' charge for the clinics. No one yet knew whether Big Lick families could pay or would pay even these small sums on a regular basis sufficient to support a nurse and the occasional doctors' visits. They had funds for a building and its maintenance, but as yet no assured source of financial support for a program. A lot was riding on Gene Smathers's leadership, and he was, by his own admission, "almost totally ignorant of such health centers and their work."

The health center was constructed the same way as the church. Beginning in August of 1937, the same mason and the people of Big Lick worked through the winter, pausing as necessary for the weather, a total of 140 days. Gene Smathers was there every day, and Loucile donated twenty-four days of labor. A total of eighty-two individuals representing forty-nine of the fifty-four families that comprised the Big Lick community contributed labor on the building, a 91 percent participation rate. This was more than twice the number that had contributed to the building of the church. Their donated labor and materials were valued at $1,400, a little more than 30 percent of the total cost of the building. They finished by the middle of May 1938, and on June 22, 1938, the building was dedicated as the Warren H. Wilson House of Health.

The health center was a sparkling addition to the community. Even beyond the church, it was the finest structure and most comfortable residence in the community. It was well equipped and up-to-date. It was completely wired for electricity supplied by a diesel-powered Delco generator and had hot and cold running water and a full bathroom with two water supplies. In addition to a cistern, there was a deep well powered by an electric pump. The well provided pure potable water, and the cistern system routed rainwater through an activated charcoal filter and provided water for everything except drinking and cooking.

One end of the first floor and all the second floor provided living quarters for a nurse and an assistant. The other end of the first floor contained a waiting room, a fully equipped examination room, a small lab, and a ward with two hospital beds. The ward was dedicated to the Smatherses' infant son who had died and was furnished through gifts from friends of the family. The living quarters included a living room, a large kitchen, a dining room, and three bedrooms upstairs. The living room was finished in wood paneling and included a large stone fireplace.

At the dedication service, Gene Smathers spoke quite personally, saying, "An occasion such as this is both a time of joy and of sadness." He spoke then briefly about Dr. Warren H. Wilson and his contribution to rural mission work and the ministry at Big Lick in particular. He said that Dr. Wilson "believed most of all in the sanctity of three things: the soil, the lives of poor people, and the worship of God in small intimate groups ... and saw our House of Health as an expression of his belief in the lives of country folk, that is, with his belief that they are worth as much as their city brothers and deserve adequate opportunities."[3]

He spoke of how he personally had

> worked hard and faced disappointments... My contributions are a personal memorial to Dr. Wilson who meant much to me as a friend and counselor. Also a second memorial to our infant son, Charles. These two, one whose life spanned only 10 months—the other 69 years—will be closely associated in memory. Dr. Wilson baptized Charles and his message of sympathy at his death was most meaningful. While there is no tablet to remind you that our part is a memorial [to our] son, yet I hope that down through the years, the wider community of this place and the lives of little children will be revived. You who live here and share this ministry [will know] that in part this building stands here because a pastor and his wife lost a son, and they have given of their best to give other children an opportunity for health and development."[4]

In his foreword to the booklet _Worth a Pound of Cure - a Short History of the Warren H. Wilson House of Health, Big Lick, Tennessee_, Mike Smathers wrote,

Its formal name was the Warren H. Wilson House of Health. We called it simply "the Health Center" (pronounced "Helz Center"). It was one of the structures and institutions that defined the world for those of us who grew up in Big Lick in the 1940s and 50s. We went to the doctor there. We had our health checkups there. We got out shots there. Some of us had our tonsils taken out there. A few of us were born there. We harassed the nurses and teachers who lived there. But we never paid much attention to how or why it came to be, or the role it was playing in shaping the society around us.[5]

"Well Baby Clinic at new Health Center - 1938"

"A Pound of Cure"

Measured against the ambitious dreams and expectations of its founders, especially Wilson and Smathers, the Big Lick health program was never fully a success. Its early success depended upon the cooperation of some of the Crossville doctors, and for a time, two of the better local physicians did staff the two monthly clinics. Then the majority of the County Medical Association censured those two doctors and adopted a resolution forbidding any of their members from working with such a low-cost or free or subscription (or "socialist" as some called it) health care delivery system. Those two doctors had to cease and desist their aid to the Big Lick clinics under threat of losing their medical license.[6]

After some floundering around, Smathers was able to secure the assistance of two missionary doctors, Dr. May Cravath Wharton and Dr. Margaret Kesler Stewart, who were based in Pleasant Hill, Tennessee, and as osteopaths were not members of the County Medical Association. In any case, they essentially saved the Big Lick health program by agreeing to staff the two monthly Big Lick clinics. Dr. Wharton is famous in this region for her pioneering medical work and advocacy for a hospital in Crossville.[7] She would later work with Smathers and others to establish several "cooperative" health centers in other communities around the county as well as to build a hospital in Crossville.

In the spring of 1939, Smathers thought Big Lick had the situation solved permanently when he and the community made plans to settle a refugee doctor at the health center. They had a plan for supporting the doctor with sufficient food and other necessities until the health program began to generate some revenue. They had contact with several "suitable doctors" who were willing to come. This plan was specifically targeted and killed by what Smathers called a "dictatorial ruling" of the Tennessee Board of Medical Examiners that no doctor who was not a graduate of an American medical college could practice in the state. Big Lick's plans were derailed by what Smathers called a "head-on with the AMA."[8]

The persistent opposition of the local and state medical associations was not the only problem that plagued the health center and the Big Lick health program. Funding was never secure. Nurses came and went too frequently. There were long stretches when no nurse could be secured to live at the health center and oversee the health program. It had resident nurses for only eight of the thirty years it functioned as a community facility. The two planned monthly clinics occurred regularly for only fourteen of those thirty years. Like the biblical Jubilee, the planned subscription health program surfaced for only brief and intermittent periods and never worked as had been hoped.

On the other hand, the health center and the community health program succeeded in ways unforeseen by its planners and to an extent beyond the wildest dreams and most fervent hopes of its founders. It found its success in its role as an example and an inspiration. During the fourteen years it functioned as a community health facility more or less as it had been planned, over six hundred visitors from at least thirty states and fifteen foreign countries came to see and learn from the work being done in Big Lick. It will never be known how many community health programs throughout the world were inspired, informed, and influenced by the little health center at Big Lick that never really succeeded.

Closer to home, however, it is known that the health center and the Big Lick health program played a significant role in improving and expanding health services in Cumberland County, and in helping Dr. May Cravath Wharton fulfill her dream of establishing a hospital in the county seat of Crossville.

The final chapter of Dr. Wharton's autobiography opens with this excerpt:

> Dr. May, said Mr. White, stopping me in the hall one day, do you remember the article I wrote for 'The Classmate' some time ago? Oh, about the Big Lick Coops. Miss Goodale and I read it and liked it very much.
>
> Well, here's a letter from Dr. R. M. Metcalfe of Rochester, Minnesota. He read it and wants to know more about the area. Says he is seeking a rural location, especially one where cooperative medicine might work. Shall I tell him about Uplands?
>
> Of course, Mr. White. Invite him to come and look us over if he's really interested.

Mr. White did write. He found that Dr. Metcalfe was a specialist in internal medicine, finishing two years of service at the Mayo Clinic. He was looking for a challenging permanent location, and he liked the South. Their correspondence was a lively one. I joined in, and within a few months Dr. Metcalfe and his wife came down to see us.[9]

There is a story behind Dr. May's excerpt that is not fully fleshed out in her book. Mr. White was the Reverend Edwin White, a Congregationalist minister at Pleasant Hill, Tennessee, who in late1945 had written an article about cooperative efforts, including a cooperative subscription health program developed by a Presbyterian church in Big Lick, Tennessee. The article was published in a Methodist Sunday school magazine (*The Classmate*) and read by Dr. Robert Metcalfe and his wife Ethel in Rochester, Minnesota. What caught the Metcalfes' eyes and piqued their interest in the Cumberland County area was what was happening with cooperatives, including a health cooperative, at Big Lick.

Dr. May was certainly influential in convincing the Metcalfes to settle in Cumberland County. But what she does not say in her autobiography (presumably because she did not know it and her autobiography is, after all, her story) was that the single most influential factor in the Metcalfes' decision was the work that was going on at Big Lick under the leadership of Gene Smathers. This is known by Dr. Metcalfe's own testimony at an installation service for the author as pastor of Calvary Presbyterian Church of Big Lick on August 19, 1979. It was Smathers's success with cooperatives and Smathers's experience with an alternative type of health care delivery system as much as Dr. Mays' advocacy and gentle persuasion that convinced the Metcalfes to settle in Cumberland County.

Dr. May does go on in her autobiography to note how quickly the pace of activity sped up after Dr. Metcalfe arrived at Uplands in October 1946. She notes how his administrative skills and knowledge of advanced medical and hospital methods quickly shaped up the planning for a new hospital in Crossville. She notes his skill at attracting other health professionals to join a team he was assembling. What she does not talk about is the time that Dr. Metcalfe spent talking, corresponding with, and collaborating with Gene Smathers.

From the first time they met, Gene Smathers and Bob Metcalfe liked each other. They discovered that they thought alike a lot, including about what health care and health care facilities should look like in a rural area. Smathers's experience and success with cooperatives helped Metcalfe believe that some type of cooperative health care system could be developed in Cumberland County. Shortly after Dr. Metcalfe arrived at Uplands in 1946, Gene Smathers was invited to join the Upland's Board. Metcalfe helped to get Smathers named chairman of the first countywide health council in 1948. Both these actions were instrumental in pushing along the planning for a new hospital in Crossville. Smathers served continuously on the Uplands Board from 1946 to 1963 when he resigned. Then in 1966, he joined the Board of the Uplands Cumberland Medical Center in Crossville.

With his contacts and charisma, Dr. Metcalfe was soon able to assemble around him a team of doctors and other health professionals that formed the Cumberland Clinic Foundation where doctors were on salary and patients could pay according to a sliding scale. Some of these doctors (e.g., Marion Young) had known Smathers before they knew Metcalfe. The monthly clinics at Big Lick were reestablished and staffed by the Cumberland Clinic doctors. With the help of Dr. May, similar clinics were established at other locations around the county.

Dr. May is rightly credited with being the visionary who first saw the need for a hospital in Crossville that would adequately serve the whole county, and she is the one that spent a good portion of her life working to see this dream fulfilled. However, without the charisma and the medical and organizational skills of Bob Metcalfe and the leadership talents of Gene Smathers, along with the efforts of other farsighted and dedicated citizens, it is unlikely that she would have seen that dream fulfilled.

When the Big Lick Health Center ceased to function as a health facility in the mid 1950s, it died not so much because of its failures as because of its successes. The Cumberland Medical Center, the Cumberland Clinic, the overall improvement of health services in Crossville, along with improved roads, had made a community health facility such as the Warren H. Wilson House of Health unnecessary.

NOTES

1. Smathers, *"I Work in the Cumberlands,"* op. cit., 6 in pamphlet; 4 in *Rural America* article.
2. Ibid, Smathers, "I Work in the Cumberlands,' 5 and 7 in pamphlet; 3 and 4 in *Rural America* article.
3. Eugene Smathers, dedicatory speech at dedication of the Warren H.
4. Wilson House of Health, June 22, 1938.
5. Ibid, Smathers, Dedicatory Speech.
6. Judy Smathers and Nora Beck, *Worth a Pound of Cure*, booklet compiled by Judy Smathers and Nora Beck and published privately by the Calvary Church Homestead Project, 2002.
7. Gene Smathers always considered it an accomplishment of the Big Lick health program that a significant number of the young women in the Calvary Church congregation became nurses. This, however, was not among the original objectives of the health center and its program.
8. See May Cravath Wharton, MD, *Doctor Woman of the Cumberlands: The Autobiography of May Cravath Wharton, MD*, published by Uplands, Pleasant Hill, Tennessee, 1953, 1973, and 2001.
9. Paradoxically by 1950, the AMA was inviting Gene Smathers to a national conference to consider the issue of rural health service. Wharton, op. cit., *Doctor Woman...*, 201.

CHAPTER 6

PUTTIN' BREAD ON THE TABLE

By the fall of 1938, the Depression had dropped average family incomes in Big Lick to under $50 per year. Only those who had gotten on with the WPA had any real income. Over the years, Gene Smathers had tried several things to improve the economic situation without much success. "A 'Farmers School' was tried," he later remembered, "and 'experts' at considerable effort prescribed ways for making a better income, but nothing much happened."[1]

Then in the winter of 1938, he discovered a "study-for-action" technique that he thought "promised definite results." Known colloquially as the "study clubs," it had been developed in Nova Scotia primarily by a Roman Catholic priest with the appropriate name of Moses Coady. More formally known as the "Antigonish Movement" (after the town in Nova Scotia where it was centered), it fit neatly into Smathers's ideology. It promised democratic governance by the people themselves and cooperative economic development.[2]

Like Gene Smathers, Coady believed fervently that it was the right and responsibility of common people to initiate and control the economic structures that shape their lives. They both believed that ordinary people should be the masters of their own destiny. Coady was suspicious of capitalism, considered labor unions untrustworthy, and was an avowed opponent of socialism. He was searching for what would come to be called in Canada a "middle way" between capitalism and socialism. He believed, again like Smathers, that any method of economic development had to be based on Christian ethics and social justice.[3]

Both Smathers and Coady were advocates of adult education. One of Smathers's often quoted aphorisms was "If given the right information and an opportunity to learn from each other, common people can solve their own problems." Like the folks in Nova Scotia, the people of Big Lick felt a kind of "economic helplessness," and like Coady, Smathers believed it was his job to help them organize to challenge this apparent helplessness.

The study club method of community economic development was highly democratic—the membership was self-selected, they elected their own leaders, and if outside experts were used, they came in to answer the clubs' questions or to advise the club members about the economic development techniques that the club had chosen to implement. Moreover, these solutions often involved the use of cooperative economic enterprises (whether they were called cooperatives or not). Big Lick became the first community in the Southern Appalachians to try study clubs.

In a letter dated December 12, 1939, Smathers tells briefly of Big Lick's early experience with study clubs:

> During the winter of 1938-39, the [Study Club] idea was presented to a community meeting and there was good response. Two Study Clubs, patterned after Nova Scotia, meeting each Wednesday evening in the homes of the members, were started. Each group elected its own leader from among their number and selected a subject or subjects for study. The subjects selected grew out of their 'bread and butter', needs [that is] their [immediate] economic needs. Once each month, we had a combined meeting when each group reported its problems and conclusions . . .
>
> One group chose as its subject, "cattle," the other chose the "cooperative buying of farm supplies," having the purchase

of fertilizer especially in mind . . . This study did result in a small cooperative fertilizer buying project, but an even more important thing developed.

During the discussion of this Study Club, the problem of inadequate farming equipment came to the fore and the men began to study about some practical way of meeting it. Our farms are small and our incomes very low, making it impossible for the individual farmer to own personally all the tools which he needs. Out of this need came the idea of a Farmers' Association. (We did not call it a cooperative association for special local reasons, although it is that) . . . The tool most needed was a grain drill, so the first questions centered around this tool. But this [Study Club] soon saw the wisdom of making our organization much broader in scope. So a plan for a simple farmers' cooperative was worked out, true to cooperative principles in every respect and broad enough to include many possible activities. Although it was determined that the first task was the purchasing of a grain drill and certain other tools, as capital was available.[4]

At another time in another issue of *Religious Education*, Smathers explained the process this way, claiming that it too was a part of "religious education":

A few small farmers are sitting around the fire in a neighbor's home. They are members of a study group wrestling with some of their common problems, and at the moment are concerned with the need for more adequate farm machinery . . . which none as individual farmers can afford . . . yet which all need . . . to become more effective on their small, hillside farms . . . The suggestion is made that the group consider the cooperative technique as a solution of their problem. So for several meetings the group studies the principles of cooperatives and work on a set of by-laws [for] their local association. Finally the by-laws are ready

> and . . . are [to be presented] to a larger gathering of farmer neighbors . . . Several agree to become charter members of the little association. It takes real faith in the purposes of the organization and in their fellow members for these men to pay the membership fees, for their cash resources are almost non-existent.[5]

The capital needed to purchase the grain drill was raised by membership fees of $10 each and by gift memberships. The church took a membership, and several groups from supporting churches took out gift memberships. The $10 membership fee represented as much as 20 percent of the annual cash income of some of the members, so they made it possible to pay the membership fee over time. They were soon able to purchase a grain drill. This drill made it possible for each farmer to plant up to ten times as much corn as they could previously. The drill was rented to members, thereby raising additional capital for other purchases. In a relatively short time, they had also purchased a one-horse corn drill and a tooth harrow.

Soon the second study club decided to build a cooperative dipping vat for cattle (a devise that enabled them to treat their livestock for ticks and lice that can rob livestock of as much as 20 percent of their body weight and energy). From this beginning, the Farmer's Association continued to grow until it owned a large tractor, several pieces of tractor equipment, a hammer mill for making animal feed from corn, and a small mill for the grinding of flour and cornmeal for home use. As it grew, it provided a part-time job for one person as an operator and mechanic. It served the community for over thirty years.

At the same time, the farmers continued to purchase lime and fertilizer in bulk on a cooperative basis. The next year (1940), they established a cooperative sawmill, which provided jobs for eight men and two teams and permitted anyone in the community to get timber sawed into useful lumber at a reasonable price and close to home. The sawmill never became the thriving enterprise that its founders thought it might, but it did serve the community for over twenty years. Several homes and many farm buildings were built with lumber sawed at the cooperative mill. By cooperative marketing, many community residents were able to market the small amount of timber they had on their places, thus bringing in additional cash income. As Gene Smathers wrote, "[All this] is being handled in fine shape by the 'study club' technique of pooled wisdom and effort."[6]

The study clubs not only led to cooperative action, but each participant also learned from others and that pooled wisdom was put into practice on individual farms. Smathers quotes a local County Agricultural Extension agent who wrote to Smathers:

> Six months of study in a special agricultural school away from home could not have done the things for many of the farmers in your Big Lick community which they have done themselves in a year of Study Club under your leadership. They now come to my office seeking information to use in making farm problem decisions and community decisions like no other community.
>
> Through the Study Club, Big Lick families are learning by searching out information on their problems from the best sources. They send committees out to study and report on problems, then action is taken by the group. This is truly democracy at work . . . Big Lick is setting a pattern for surrounding communities.[7]

A credit union was tried, the first in the Southern Appalachian region, without much success because no one had any money to put into it. Three other cooperative enterprises were later attempted without much success either. The first was a strawberry marketing cooperative, and the second a bell pepper marketing coop. While they lasted, these programs provided some supplemental income to both farmers who grew the berries and peppers and to the many people who helped harvest them.

These programs were killed in a few years by the competition from California growers who benefitted from two federally authorized projects (one of them federally funded). One was the completion of a portion of the San Joaquin Valley irrigation project, which provided year-round water to that portion of California's Central Valley. The second was the Bracero Program, which ran from 1942 to 1964 and permitted California farmers to contract and import labor from Mexico. These two programs combined to enable California farmers to produce, harvest, and ship strawberries and bell peppers year-round at a cost below what it cost Tennessee farmers to grow them.

A second abortive cooperative endeavor grew out of the post-WWII phenomenon of backyard barbecuing. At that time, charcoal was the primary fuel used for this purpose. And charcoal production provided the farmer an outlet for low-grade hardwoods and brush from land clearing that otherwise had little or no value. In fact, it was merely a nuisance since it had to be burned anyway. Big Lick's answer to the need for charcoal was the Daddy's Creek Charcoal Producers Inc. The idea was that farmers would produce charcoal during the winter using low-value timber, and then they would market the charcoal cooperatively in the summer. They needed to market cooperatively because no one of the small farmers involved could produce enough charcoal in a season to be commercially viable.

The charcoal was packaged in ten-pound sacks and marketed throughout the Southeast. In 1953, the going wholesale price for the packaged product was $60 per ton FOB Big Lick, and the Daddy's Creek Producers sold eighty-five tons to locations in Tennessee, Alabama, Kentucky, Illinois, and South Carolina. However, the enterprise was short-lived.

Part of the reason for its demise lay at the feet of its organizers. They never did solve the problem of storing the charcoal in bulk or in packaged form during the winter months when there was no market for it. However, what really led to its downfall was the invention of the charcoal briquette. About the time the Daddy's Creek Producers was ready to go into full operation, the bottom fell out of the market for loose (nonbriquette) charcoal.

The study clubs and the cooperatives they spawned also developed the leadership skills of those who participated in them. As was true for the health program, the Big Lick cooperatives, even in their failures, had a wider impact. Later in the 1940s, the leadership skills gained and the knowledge learned by the Big Lick cooperators made them a valuable asset in the organization of a countywide farmers' cooperative that is still a going concern today in 2014.

Gene Smathers served often as an officer of the Cumberland Farmer's Cooperative. He was chairman of its board of directors in 1967 when he was elected moderator of the general assembly of the United Presbyterian Church. It is believed that he is the only person ever to serve simultaneously as moderator of the general assembly and chairman of a local farmers' cooperative, though he relinquished the latter post to another Big Lick cooperative leader shortly after being elected moderator.

"Study Club Meeting – 1939"

"Gene Smathers scaling logs at sawmill – 1940"

NOTES

1. Eugene Smathers, "The Contribution of the Church to Big Lick Community," *Religious Education* (January–February), 955: 3.
2. See Anne Alexander, *The Antigonish Movement*, Thompson Educational Publishing, Inc., Toronto, 1997; also see M. M. Coady, *Masters of Their Own Destiny,* Harper and Brothers, October 4, 1939. For more specifically on the relationship of cooperatives to religion, see M. M. Coady, "Cooperation and Religion," *The Christian Rural Fellowship Bulletin*, 50, (March 1940).
3. Ibid, Alexander and Coady
4. Eugene Smathers, letter to Benson Y. Landis, December 12, 1939.
5. Eugene Smathers, "Religious Education and the Spiritual Values of Rural life," *Religious Education* 40, no. 2 (March–April 1945), 70–71.
6. Eugene Smathers, "I Work in the Cumberlands," op. cit., 12 in pamphlet; 6 in *Rural America* article.
7. Ibid, Smathers 13–14 in pamphlet; 6 in *Rural America* article.

CHAPTER 7

THE CALVARY CHURCH HOMESTEAD PROJECT

On January 29, 1940, Gene Smathers wrote to L. C. Armstrong:

> The Berkshire boar arrived safely on Jan. 24 and the sow pigs came the 26th. All are very fine hogs, and we are much pleased with them . . . The night the pigs arrived the temperature reached what I suspect is an all-time low for our area, 30 below zero. We have had sub-zero weather for almost two weeks. It was 20 below Sunday A.M. . . .
>
> We brought the pigs into our living room the night they arrived and gave them their first food and water in Big Lick.[1]

The boar and piglets would initiate the next project of the Big Lick Farmers Association—an effort to improve the quality of hogs raised by Big Lick Farmers. This feedstock was provided by a men's Sunday school class in Westfield, New Jersey, of which Mr. Armstrong was a leader.

Never mind the record-breaking cold or the new Berkshire hogs, Gene Smathers's mind was already off on a more ambitious undertaking. On December 12, 1939, at the end of a letter primarily about the Big Lick cooperatives, Smathers wrote to Benson Y. Landis in New York:

> We are also in the beginning of the development of a church sponsored land settlement project, which will have cooperative features. Our community is surrounded by unsettled land and at the same time we have a group of young people who [are] dammed up here, with little educational or vocational opportunity. We plan to secure some of this land and give these youth an opportunity to own a farm and home of their own. I see this project as one of great value *but* the details are not fully worked-out at the present time.

Throughout 1939, there had been a long series of letters between Smathers; Charles Greenway of the Board of National Missions; James W. Brown, Big Lick's benefactor for the church and health center; and Don Fessler, a rural development specialist that the Board of National Missions brought in to assist and advise in the development of a land-settlement project sponsored by Calvary Church. By September 1939, a tentative plan was in place, and Fessler had even drawn up an outline to make it a national project.

It would be a capitalist land reform project, pure and simple. The project would purchase large tracts of undeveloped absentee-owned land, subdivide it into farm-sized parcels, and sell it by a liberal long-term contract. Big Lick was an island of small land parcels surrounded by a sea of large absentee-owned tracts of land. The owners of these tracts were unwilling to break them up into smaller parcels that Big Lick families might purchase. Even if the owners had been so inclined, no young Big Lick family could have gotten the funds (by loan or otherwise) to purchase the parcels.

On November 9, 1939, Brown visited Big Lick for face-to-face talks with Smathers about the plan. The next day, Brown wrote a letter to Greenway, enclosing $4,500 to establish in Big Lick what was initially called the "James W. Brown Farm Settlement Fund." On November 18, Smathers received a letter from Greenway informing him of the fund. However, the fund was to be controlled by the Board of National Missions. Smathers would have almost as much trouble working out the final operational details of the project with the church bureaucracy as the nearby Cumberland Homesteaders had with the federal bureaucracy.

By March 1940, Smathers was frantic to get the money for he had options to buy from several absentee landowners and his options were about to expire. On March 27, he wrote to Greenway, urgently requesting that the funds be sent immediately. He received a telegraph reply that the money was on the way. However, individual checks had to be approved and written for each seller in New York, and it was not until April 4 that he actually received the checks. He was able to purchase four tracts of land that would begin what by then was being called the "Calvary Church Homestead Project." The four tracts totaled 409.3 acres and were purchased for $3,352.60. One proposed tract was lost because of the delay.

The Board of National Missions wished to maintain control of the project in New York although the board explicitly took no responsibility for financial support of the project and did not formally approve it until their meeting of April 25–26, 1940. Technically and legally, the project was a project of the Board of National Missions with Eugene Smathers authorized to act as trustee on behalf of the board. On the ground in Big Lick, the project operated as a function of Calvary Presbyterian Church. There was a board of trustees composed of three elders of the church along with Smathers. Another elder served as escrow agent.

Smathers never made decisions about the selection of homesteaders or the acquisition or sale of land without the approval of the full local board of trustees. All deeds were signed by these trustees. However, for several years, all funds were retained by the board in New York and all checks had to be written there and signed by board officials. Smathers was required to file quarterly reports to the board on all expenditures, all receipts from homesteaders, and the progress of all homesteaders. Getting the funds approved and the checks signed and delivered to Big Lick often took longer than Smathers thought prudent or necessary. This cumbersome and time-consuming process was a source of some friction between Smathers and the board until sometime in the 1950s when, at the urging of Smathers, the board ceased their involvement, turned over all funds to the local trustees, and allowed the project to become fully a function of Calvary Presbyterian Church.

"Typical Big Lick house before the Homestead Project – 1940"

The Calvary Church Homestead Plan was straightforward. Land was sold to the homesteader on a thirty-year contract with quarterly (or less frequent) payments that bore interest at 3 percent. Payments were expected to come from income earned from the farm. The 3 percent interest was to be used to pay the administrative costs of the project with any excess to be applied toward community-improvement projects. Land was sold at cost (including the costs of any improvements made to the property while it was owned by the project). No one drew any salary or income from the operation of the project. Simultaneously, with the contract of sale (called an escrow agreement), the project trustees executed a deed to the homesteader. This deed was not recorded but was held by the escrow agent until the homesteader had met the terms of the contract.

Unlike most "land contracts," the Calvary Church Homestead Project "escrow agreement" provided for repayment of a portion of the principal the homesteader had paid, plus the appraised value of any improvements the homesteader had made in the event the homesteader found it necessary to leave the land and relinquish the deed to the project trustees. This provision was at the discretion of the project trustees, but it was interpreted very liberally. Most of the homesteaders who found it necessary to move from their land for any reason (such as securing a better-paying job at another location) were able to "sell" their homestead back to the project and receive back some of the cash they had put into it. Otherwise, the homesteader could not sell or transfer any interest in the property to a third party without the approval of the project trustees.

In certain circumstances, the payment period could be extended for more than thirty years with the homesteader required to pay only the interest during the intervening years. Also, a variable payment plan was possible whereby the homesteader could pay more in good crop years and less in bad crop years. Each homesteader was also given a membership in the Big Lick Farmer's Association. In addition, homesteaders could borrow money from the homestead fund at 5 percent interest to improve their house, to purchase livestock, or to undertake other farm improvements approved by the project trustees.

Land reform it was, but it was land reform with strings. The real "kicker" in the contract was the requirement that the homesteader abide by certain land-use practices. These included the following:

1. Participation in the Soil Conservation Program of the Cumberland County AAA.
2. Adopting a system of crop rotation.
3. Land too steep for cultivation had to be maintained in woodland or permanent pasture.

4. Planting of cultivatable land with winter cover crops.
5. Conservation and use of the manure produced on the farm. Grain residue (cornstalks) and other crop refuse could not be burned but was to be returned to the soil.
6. The first purpose of the homesteaders' farm produce was to provide sufficient food for the family and for livestock on the farm. Only after that was accomplished was the farmer allowed to sell any of his farm produce.

Homesteaders were also "expected" (not required) "to participate in all farm and community meetings, to take advantage of opportunities to improve their knowledge of and skill in the best farm practices, and cooperate in enterprises for general community improvement." Moreover, the land could only be used for farming, and in the event that a homesteader had to sell his property back to the project, he or she* could not receive any "speculative" increase in the value of the land.

Sometime in the 1950s, a comparison was made between the federally sponsored Cumberland Homestead six miles away and the Calvary Church Homestead Project. It concluded that (1) Calvary homesteaders' farmsteads were larger in general (and therefore more likely sustainable); (2) Calvary homesteaders were able to acquire ownership of their farms more cleanly and quickly; and (3) Calvary Homesteaders were treated more equitably in the event they had to leave their farm. Cumberland Homesteaders had a firmer non-farm employment base and a larger, therefore more sustainable, community. (The Cumberland Homesteaders were finally forced to get a special act of Congress passed before they could acquire ownership of their farmsteads.)[2]

Two needs permeated Gene Smathers's vision for the Calvary Church Homestead Project. The first of these was the need of young men and young families who had no cash and no way of purchasing sufficient land for farms from large absentee landowners (or even from

---

* At least one single woman homesteaded a tract of land.

their neighbors who might have extra land to sale). They could not acquire sufficient land on which to establish a viable farm and thereby make a living. The second need was the long-term viability of the community and the church. If all these young men and families were forced to leave the community in order to establish a livelihood, what would eventually happen to the community and the church?

One of the needs Smathers had not anticipated but which emerged immediately as soon as funds were available was the need to help those who already owned farms to keep their farms. Some of the first loans made from the homestead fund were to farmers who were at risk of losing their farm for failure to pay taxes or inability to make loan payments. In these situations, the project purchased the farm for $1, paid off the note that was owed on it, and resold it to the farmer under a homesteader contract. The farmer paid the project only the amount of taxes or loan paid off by the homestead project.

There can be little question that the Calvary Church Homestead Project saved the community of Big Lick and Calvary Church. The two hundred or so families helped to date by the Calvary Church Homestead Project have formed and continue to form the backbone of the Big Lick community and Calvary Church. The project has changed with the years and is no longer engaged in purchasing vacant land, cutting it up into subsistence farmsteads and selling it by long-term contract to future farmers. It still exists as of 2014, but as the community and needs have changed, it has changed so that it now primarily assists families to purchase or improve homes. As of March 2014, it has seven families that are building, purchasing, or improving homes with assistance from the project.

"Typical Big Lick house after the Homestead Project – 1960"

All the funds to initiate the project came from Big Lick's primary benefactor, James Wilson Brown. Between 1940 and 1950, Mr. Brown gave a total of $32,228.25 to initiate and expand the Calvary Church Homestead Project, the largest amount he put into any of the Big Lick projects. As of March 2014, that corpus has grown to $285,853.37. In addition, much of the interest has gone to church and community-improvement projects including a new Sunday school building, the building of a new manse at the church, a cafeteria in the local school as long as it was retained as a community school, a small park at the church, and improvements in the community cemetery.

NOTES

[1] According to those with radios, the National Weather Service reported that at 30 below zero, Crossville, Tennessee, was the coldest spot in the nation on January 26, 1940. January 24-27, 1940, was also the last time the Cumberland River froze over at Nashville, Tennessee.

[2] Mike Smathers, "The Search for the Garden," _Southern Exposure_ 8, no. 1 (Spring 1980), 57–63.

CHAPTER 8

THE SCHOLAR

Valedictorian of his high school class (the other senior was salutatorian), graduated in three years from Transylvania University while holding down a regular job and playing varsity tennis, graduated magna cum laude from the seminary, the only senior to graduate with honors in three different subjects: Gene Smathers had always been a scholar.

"I love books," he wrote to Loucile during their courtship by correspondence. "I already have quite a few, but a fellow can never have too many. It's one thing when you are at a place that has a library, but when a fellow gets out on his own, he has to depend upon himself." From 1927–1967, it is estimated that he read all or parts of fifty to one hundred books per year. At his death, he had over five thousand books in his personal library, and he had read at least parts of most of them.

It was an eclectic collection. He owned or had on loan from time to time books by the most up-to-date theologians and the most-renowned preachers of the day. He had dozens of books on the role of the pastor. However, he had an equal number of books, if not more, on agriculture, soil conservation, community and economic development, cooperatives, and related subjects. He had books on how to build a sermon and on how to build a hog house. He owned and had read a complete set of Reinhold Niebuhr's works and a full set of the *Yearbook of Agricultural* published annually by the USDA. Books on how to mix fertilizers, along with histories and biographies (Churchill on WWII, Sandburg on Lincoln); exposés such as *The American Way of Death*, *Let Us Now Praise Famous Men*, *Silent Spring*; novels by Twain, Melville, Steinbeck, Salinger, Fitzgerald, Orwell, and others; cartoons by Bill Mauldin; books of poetry by Robert Frost and Langston Hughes were all found on his shelves.

To get a feel for the range and contemporaneousness of his reading, consider the following *partial* list of books he read from 1965–1967 (the last years he had time for extensive reading). Only the books that could be positively identified as having been read during this period are included in this list. They represent probably 15 to 25 percent of his total reading for this period. These books show signs of being carefully read with extensive underlining and marginal notes. Dates of publication are shown in parentheses ().

- *Stinking Creek* by John Fetterman (1967) – an anthropological study of an Appalachian neighborhood.
- *The Secular City* by Harvey Cox (1965) – sociology/theology.
- *Yesterday's People* by Jack Weller (1966) – a sociological analysis of Appalachian people.
- *Acquittal by Resurrection* by Markus Barth and Verne H. Fletcher (1964) – biblical studies/theology.
- *Free in Obedience* by William Stringfellow (1964) – theology.
- *a Private and a Public Faith* by William Stringfellow (1964) – theology.
- *Dissenter in a Great Society* by William Stringfellow (1966) – theology.
- *The Death of God* by Thomas J. J. Altizer and William Hamilton (1966) - theology.
- *Prophet of Plenty* by Wilma Dykeman (1966) – Biography of W. D. Weatherford, Southern Appalachian education pioneer.
- *Freedom and Order* by Henry Steele Commager (1966) – political science.

- *Southern White Protestantism in the Twentieth Century* by Kenneth K. Bailey (1964) – ecclesiology.
- *Southern Churches in Crisis* by Samuel S. Hill Jr. (1966) – ecclesiology.
- *Manchild in the Promised Land* by Claude Brown (1965) – autobiography, black studies.
- *Situation Ethics: The New Morality* by Joseph Fletcher (1966) – ethics.
- *The Church Inside Out* by J. C. Hoekendijk (1966) – ecclesiology.
- *God's Frozen People* by Mark Gibbs and T. Ralph Morton (1965) – general Christianity.

"Gene Smathers in his study with Buffy – 1950s"

Smathers thought he had forsaken an academic career when he left the seminary and turned his back on his professors' advice to attend graduate school in 1932. However, an opportunity came looking for him in 1942. The first historical record of it is buried in Smathers's journal entry for Wednesday, March 11, 1942. In a note about his attendance (along with three others from Big Lick) at a conference in Knoxville, he wrote, "Saw Dr. [Henry] Randolph [of the Board of National Missions] who dropped bombshell re possibility of working at Vanderbilt School of Religion in rural church work. Later had a brief conversation with Dean Denton [*sic*] re same . . . It is raining again today - so no plowing this week." (Note: The dean's name was Benton, not Denton.)

If truth be told, that 1932 decision had been partly financial. He was already in debt from the seminary and did not know how he would get money for graduate school. He was an excellent teacher. It was, after all, the Religious Education Prize that he had won upon seminary graduation. He always taught an adult Sunday school at his churches and believed that he made more progress with his teaching than he did in his preaching.

Smathers was already recognized as a scholar in the field of church and community, having produced over a dozen articles, pamphlets, book chapters, and lectures on the subject. He was also recognized for his expertise in community and economic development and in the role of the church in rural reconstruction. He would only later become recognized as an authority on soil stewardship and conservation on which he would also write and lecture extensively.

So Smathers was enticed and challenged by the possibility of teaching at Vanderbilt. On March 27, 1942, Dean John Keith Benton and another Vanderbilt faculty member visited Smathers at his home in Big Lick. Benton is reputed to have said upon leaving Smathers's study, "That man has more books in his study than any minister I have ever seen." The other faculty member replied, "And what's more, he appears to have read all of them." Whether that conversation is apocryphal or true, it does not state a true fact. Smathers had not read *all* the books in his library. But it is fair to say that he had read, skimmed, or read parts of most of them.

By May 1942, details of an arrangement had been worked out. Smathers told his parishioners about it in the May-June issue (vol. 5, nos. 8 and 9) of the parish newsletter, *Calvary Fellowship*. There, he wrote,

"This year will bring a new phase in the work of your present pastor. He will begin a dual relationship, giving three days a week of 3 months to teaching in the School of Religion, Vanderbilt University, Nashville. There he will head up the work in the field of Church and Community."

His stint at Vanderbilt would last only three years, 1942–44. Each of those years he spent three days a week during the months of September to November, holding classes and advising students in Nashville. He probably was not a very good formal lecturer, but he was excellent in impromptu give-and-take, question-and-answer sessions.

Gene had taken the position with Loucile's blessing, but it must not be forgotten that whenever Gene was away during this time, Loucile, who had a one-year-old toddler and an eight-year-old to care for, had to take care of the church farm (feed and milk the cow, feed the hog and chickens, gather the eggs, sometimes help put up hay), manage all the community enterprises, and fulfill the role of pastor to the community. Although unknown for sure, it is believed that one of the reasons he left the Vanderbilt position was because of the wear and tear on Loucile. Another factor was probably that the extra work he had taken on after 1940 plus the work at Vanderbilt plus all that was still left to be done at home contributed to his own exhaustion.

However, he continued to love books and taught briefly at Scarritt College, Nashville, Tennessee, in 1951. He remained a consummate scholar until the last year of his life, when his activities as moderator of the general assembly left him little time for scholarly pursuits.

As an indicator of the systematic nature of his scholarship, consider the scanned copy of one of his early "Plans of Study" below.

Plan of Study for March 1923.

Theology - "The Humanity of God" : John Wright Buckham. Harper & Bros. 1928.

Bible - Amos. "The Twelve Minor Prophets" vol I. G.A. Smith. Doran pp. 61-210.
  " "   "   "   "   "   "   D.J. Robinson   "   d.B.
  " The Beacon Lights of Prophecy : R.C. Knudson. Meth. Bk.C. d.2.

Rel. Educ. - "R.E. in the Small Church. J.J. Hunnel. Westmnk.
  " Objectives in R.E. Vieth.

Homiletics - "What to Preach". Coffin -

History - Augustine.

CHAPTER 9

RACE RELATIONS PIONEER I

The Fellowship of Southern Churchmen 1934-1958

MAY 29, 1934: HIGHLANDER FOLK SCHOOL, MONTEAGLE, TENNESSEE: Today, a small group of churchmen, clergy and laypeople, black and white, from several different denominations gathered here to start a new organization. Highlander had begun as an effort to help promote unionization of industrial and farmworkers, sharecroppers, and small farmers. Today was the first time it had called together exclusively churchmen to support its agenda.[1]

The call for the meeting said they met "to discover and give practical expression to the historic redemptive mission" of the church as it ministered to the religious, racial, social, and economic conditions prevalent in the South at that time. Some called them radicals, but by and large, they were radical only in their devotion to the teachings of Jesus. They believed that Jesus's teachings and practices should be applied to all aspects of life, and in particular to the social, economic, and racial situation then existing in the South. Among those who met that day was Gene Smathers.

Jim Dombrowski, a Highlander staff member, helped organized this event. But the real mover and shaker behind this little band of "rabble-rousers" (as they would be called) was a thirty-year-old Methodist minister and socialist, Howard "Buck" Kester. By this time, Kester was already well known around the South for his liberal views and his interracial and prounion activities, especially his support of the miner's strike at Wilder, Tennessee. A Virginian, Kester had been reared by a Ku Klux Klan father, but had grown up to be a devout Christian and a self-described "Norman Thomas Socialist." In 1932, he had run beside Thomas as the Socialist Party candidate for Congress from Middle Tennessee. He got very few votes but outpolled Thomas in his district.

Dombrowski and Kester had invited this small group of like-minded Southern churchmen to the gathering with the intention of creating some type of organization. The exact nature of that organization was not clear in their minds, but they felt it would emerge from the meeting and its aftermath. Those invited held similar views on racism, segregation, labor unionism, and the sharecropping system then prevalent in the South, a system that kept sharecroppers, both black and white, in perpetual debt and bondage to absentee landowners. They also agreed that the church had a role to play in addressing these issues.

Smathers and Kester shared Southern roots and the opinion that Southern churches needed to become more involved in efforts to address and solve the problems of racial and labor injustice, and what Smathers called the "land tenure" issue (by which he meant both the prevailing sharecropper system and the ownership of the richest lands by a powerful few, often absentee owners). Both men had been radicalized by experiences in trying to help the starving families of striking miners, Smathers in Harlan County, Kentucky, and Kester in Wilder, Tennessee. Though they were both staunchly anti-Communist because they believed Communism to be at odds with Christian values, they both had been forced to defend themselves against the charge that they were Communist sympathizers.

Smathers and Kester did not agree on everything (Kester was a Socialist and pacifist, Smathers was neither). However, Smathers called Buck Kester a "prophet" and responded enthusiastically to his call for the meeting in Monteagle. Others present at that meeting included

Abram Nightingale; James Weldon Johnson of Fisk University; T. B. "Scotty" Cowan; A. L. DeJarnette; Franz Daniel; John Dillingham; Charles Webber; E. B."Ted" Shultz; Herbert King; J. H. Daves; and David Burgess.

What emerged from the meeting that day was a little organization named the "Conference of Younger Churchmen of the South." Those present pledged to continue meeting and to support one another in efforts to address the social, racial, labor, and economic issues around which they had met.

Smathers was enthusiastic about the organization and took an active role in it from the beginning. He served alone in a remote, isolated community in the Southern mountains, yet he yearned to exercise some influence over the larger issues he saw as debilitating the South. This organization had the potential to offer him that opportunity.

At a later meeting on November 11, 1936, they renamed themselves the "Fellowship of Southern Churchmen" and adopted a Statement of Principles, which was to be subscribed to as the "minimal requirement for membership." The Statement of Principles was a detailed twelve-page document that was meant both to attract like-minded individuals while at the same time disqualify Communists and any others who did not share the Christian convictions of the founders.

Among the more controversial items in their Statement of Principles were the following partial list of those Principles:

I.1. We condemn every agricultural system which results in the exploitation of workers . . . We would substitute for these evils collective action of farm workers and redistribution of land ownership as means of realizing the right of every man who works on the soil to eat the bread of his toil in security and peace . . .

2. We declare that it is imperative for all workers to organize and bargain collectively, without penalty or threat of reprisals, free from all intimidation and violence . . . It is our purpose, therefore, to encourage the unionization of workers and to educate our churches and communities to appreciate and defend these rights . . .

3. We seek the achievement of a cooperative commonwealth in which through ownership both workers and farmers exercise democratic control . . .

II.1. We therefore condemn any and all economic systems and institutions which result in abuse of the soil, or of mineral wealth, or of forests, or of water power, or any of the resources by which men must live. This abuse we now see in the system of land tenancy and sharecropping which because of absentee ownership and disinherited workers . . . brings despoilation [*sic*] to the soil and deprivation to those who till it . . .

2. We oppose the prevailing situation in much of the South where the most fertile lands are held by the powerful few . . .

III.1. We condemn therefore any social system which breeds or condones . . . poverty, ignorance, insecurity, hatred, exploitation . . . We denounce the subservience of religious leaders or institutions to such [systems] . . .

IV.1 . . . We accept it as our prophetic task to seek . . . the end of racial discrimination and segregation . . . We embrace our obligation and joy to live as brothers to men of every race and color . . .

2. We denounce the widespread denial of civil rights and liberties to large numbers of our people . . . This we see in the erection of economic qualifications for suffrage . . . We especially condemn the illegal methods of threat, intimidation, and violence used to prevent the exercise of these rights by members of colored races . . .

> We seek to defend . . . the exercise of full political and civil rights by all peoples regardless of race, color, or political convictions.

Though not quite equivalent to the Theological Declaration of Barman or the call to faith of the confessing church in Nazi Germany, in the South of 1936, it was a courageous statement that called upon Christians and churches to express full fidelity to the whole Gospel of Jesus Christ. It was adopted by Christians who knew that it would bring down upon them opposition, hatred, enmity, and perhaps violence.

The fellowship never became what its founders envisioned and hoped it would become. Many churchmen and women were attracted to its principles, but very few of them had the courage or convictions to sign on as members. Perhaps they were unwilling to pay a membership fee in order to be threatened, persecuted and blacklisted in their home communities.

Its membership never exceeded 500. In 1954, it had 370 members. By 1963, that number had dwindled to 96. All those members except Kester and his wife, Alice Harris Kester, and later Nelle Morton, had other full-time jobs. Many of them, including Gene Smathers, gave innumerable hours to keeping it going, but it never had enough membership or funding to field an adequate staff. Nevertheless, from 1934–1954, the Fellowship stood as one of few organizations that challenged the racial and economic injustices prevalent in the South. Fellowship meetings and conferences were one of the few places where blacks and whites met together as equals.

Kester eventually burned out and resigned (for the second time) from the executive secretary position in 1957. Smathers served repeatedly on its executive committee and as chairman during the critical years of 1954–1958. For 1957–1963, after Kester left, he served as both chairman and "interim coordinator," the nearest thing the organization had as staff during those years. During this critical period, the Fellowship struggled with competing goals. One was the development of a residential center at Black Mountain, North Carolina, and the other was increasing its membership. In the end, neither of these goals was accomplished.

After the 1954 Supreme Court decision outlawing segregation in schools, the Fellowship struggled to define its mission. And after 1957, its position as the leading Christian civil rights organization in the South was eclipsed by the emergence of the Southern Christian Leadership Conference, which had an even more charismatic leader who also happened to be African American. SCLC was able to attract large numbers of black churches and Christians, something the Fellowship had tried but failed to do.[2]

In 1963, under the leadership of another white Southern preacher and racial justice advocate, Will D. Campbell, the Fellowship morphed itself into another organization named the Committee of Southern Churchmen. Unlike the Fellowship, the committee never envisioned itself as a mass movement. It was to be limited to "no less than 30 and no more than 100 men and women, Negro and white about the South who see in the tragedy of race an opportunity for renewal within the Church." It elected Will Campbell as "preacher at large" and executive secretary.

Part of the committee's work took the form of a periodical, _Be Reconciled - Katallagete,_ which was published from 1965–1990. In this form, the work of the Fellowship was extended for at least another twenty-five years. As he had been at the beginning of the Fellowship, Gene Smathers was a charter member of the Committee of Southern Churchmen and served on its board of directors until his death.

NOTES

1. The information on Highlander, here and elsewhere in this book, comes from the author's personal knowledge. The author worked for many years with Highlander and also served a term on their board. The information on the Fellowship of Southern Churchmen comes exclusively from Eugene Smathers's papers.

2. To get some different views of the Fellowship of Southern Churchmen and those who headed it at various times, see the following. (This author knows that these authors, especially the latter two, are not always accurate in their reportage. He knows that from being present at the events or hearing direct testimony from others who were at the events reported upon in this and the next chapter. He, too, was a member of the Board of Directors of the Committee of Southern Churchmen.)

   A. John Egerton, *Speak Now Against The Day: The Generation Before the Civil Right Movement in the South*, first published by the University of North Carolina, published by arrangement with Alfred A. Knopf, Inc., 1994, pp. 125, 126, on Gene Smathers; 126, 153, 154, 161, 172, 237–8, 289, 380, 426, 447 on the Fellowship; and pp.18, 78, 124–6, 153–8, 161, 167, 172, 187, 289, 290, 295, 353, 356, 442, 447, 561 on Howard "Buck" Kester.

   B. Glenn Feldman, editor, *Before Brown: Civil Rights and White Backlash in the Modern South*, University of Alabama Press, Tuscaloosa, pp. 8, 11, 15, 17, 227–35 on the Fellowship, Gene Smathers, Nelle Morton, and Howard "Buck" Kester.

   C. Anthony P. Dunbar, *Against The Grain: Southern Radicals and Prophets 1929-1959*, University Press of Virginia, Charlottesville, pp. 59–61, 74–75, 137, 195–96, 178–80, 195–98, 207, 208,

229–32, 256–58, 259, 290n on The Fellowship; pp. 207–208, 257, 259 on Gene and Lucille [*sic*] Smathers; pp. 5–11, 14–15, 18, 19–23, 25–27, 29, 32–33, 34–40, 49–53, 61–75, 75–82, 85, 91, 98–100, 103–104, 108, 111–14, 119–20, 131, 133, 136–7, 142, 152, 168, 172, 158, 154–55 159–61, 164–66, 193–98, 207–08, 256–257 on Howard "Buck" Kester; 6–9, 11, 14, 22–26, 178–79, 207, 290n on Alice Kester (Howard's wife); and 229–30, 257, 259 on Nelle Morton.

CHAPTER 10

RACE RELATIONS PIONEER II

The Interracial Work Camps 1945-1954

JUNE 30, 1945, BIG LICK, TENNESSEE: The first work campers of the first interracial work camp ever held in the rural South arrived in Big Lick today. They will stay until August 11. There is a Hawaiian of Japanese ancestry, another Japanese American, a dark-skinned Cuban, two African Americans, and five whites in the group. During their stay, they will live together and work together as equals side by side with members of the Big Lick community.

The work camp was Nelle Morton's idea. A native East Tennessean, Morton had gained a strong sense of social justice, an opposition to racial injustice, and a dose of early feminism from her Presbyterian mother. She rode these instincts not only to college, but eventually to seminary. In1931, she became one of the earliest female graduates of a seminary, graduating with an MRE from Biblical Seminary in New York. In 1969, she would become one of the first pure feminist theologians in the country, initiating a course on "Women in the Church and Society" at Drew Seminary.[1]

Morton had long been a member of the Fellowship of Southern Churchmen (FSC). Thus when Howard "Buck" Kester "temporarily" resigned due to "exhaustion" in 1943, she took on the role as executive secretary (the primary staff position of the FSC). She served in that position until 1949 when her health forced her to resign. As executive secretary, her vision of the Fellowship differed somewhat from Kester's. Kester was an activist and had seen the Fellowship primarily as a vehicle for him and his wife to intervene "prophetically" in situations of racial and/or labor strife throughout the South. Morton, an educator, saw the FSC more as a sponsor of interracial educational events and conferences in which persons of different races could experience racial equality and serve as an example to the rest of the South.

She was two years into her position as executive secretary and three days into an FSC Creative Planning Conference at Knoxville College in Knoxville, Tennessee, when she broached the idea of work camps. The work camp idea was not new. The Quakers had sponsored work camps as early as 1866, immediately following the civil war. Then after World War I, a few international Christian organizations, associated mostly with the Quakers and the Mennonites, operated work camps as a way of helping communities recover from the ravages of war. At the same time, the work camps gave the young participants an experience of living in intentionally international collectives of college students gathered from countries that had been enemies during the war. In 1945, they were gearing up to do the same after the end of World War II.

Morton's idea was to transpose similar work camps to the South. Rather than college students from different countries, the Southern camps would be interracial and interdenominational. The work camps would include Japanese Americans as well as white and black students, and the theme would be reconciliation of the races through an experience of living and working together for a period of six weeks. They would do needed work in the host community while at the same time experiencing an interracial, interdenominational community that lived together, worked together, played together, and prayed together as equals. It was the play part that would get them in trouble.

Gene Smathers warmed to the idea immediately although he was well aware that it could be dangerous for an African American to spend more than a short time in his home community. Like many rural communities on the Cumberland Plateau, neither Big Lick nor Cumberland County had any African American citizens. The absence of African Americans did not mean an absence of intolerance and prejudice. Quite the contrary, Cumberland County had the reputation of being particularly hostile toward African Americans.

Prior to 1945, Gene Smathers already had a long history of intentionally introducing people of color to his congregation as fellow Christians. The Big Lick church had hosted visitors from India, China, the Philippines, Africa, Cuba, and other parts of the United States. Some of these were African or African American. When a visiting African American first set foot in Calvary Church of Big Lick, it was the first time that many in that congregation, especially the children, had ever seen a person with black skin.

Smathers was reasonably confident that Calvary Church was ready for a more in-depth experience in interracial living. However, he was not so confident about the communities and the county surrounding Big Lick. He vacillated for over a month, but when the FSC could find no other place in the South willing to host such a work camp, he acceded to Morton's urging and agreed to attempt hosting such a work camp. He did so with one reservation. It was essential that his church support the action.

SUNDAY, MARCH 4, 1945, CALVARY CHURCH, BIG LICK, TENNESSEE: The session and Sunday school teachers of Calvary Church met today after church for the purpose of hearing a proposal from their pastor, Eugene Smathers, about a work camp. Smathers told them that the work camp would be interracial and interdenominational. He explained some of the work that the work camp could do. After some discussion, and to Smathers great satisfaction, the session and Sunday school teachers approved the plan without a dissenting vote.[2]

On the Sundays during their stay, Calvary Church was an integrated fellowship. More significantly according to Southern taboos, beginning on Friday, July 6, and continuing every Friday evening through their departure in mid-August, they participated freely and equally with Big Lick youth in the Friday night "socials." These socials were the core of the recreation program Smathers had introduced in Big Lick. It had been Gene Smathers's ploy from the beginning to call them "socials" and what was done there "singing games" or "folk games." After all, it would have been sinful to "dance" or to hold "dances" at the church.

However, what transpired at these "socials" were folk dances—English country dances, European folk dances, and "running mountain square sets" (an up-tempo folk dance style developed in the Southern Appalachians). When they first began in the 1930s, they had no music (musicians at these affairs would have given away the fact that they really were dances), so they learned to sing and clap hands to create the music for their "singing games."

One of the first singing dances they learned was indigenous to Big Lick. It was called "Jump Josie," and for many years, it was the best remembered of the singing dances. Even in 1985, it could still be performed by a large group of old and young alike. By the 1940s, they had records for music, but many of the young people would still tell their parents that they were "going to Jump Josie." It remains a mystery how a man who could not sing or carry a tune (Smathers) was able to teach "singing games" to people who could not read music, let alone invent and introduce one that no one had ever performed before.

The ploy of the name and the great enthusiasm of the young people quieted any criticism within Smathers's church, although one matron took pride until she died that she had never been to a "social" and would never go. It need be noted that all her children attended and even became dance leaders, teaching others new dances they had learned at far away boarding schools. Other preachers in the area were not so accepting. They often criticized Calvary Church and cast curses upon the "new preacher who was leading the young people straight to Hell." This, it might be noted, did not stop the young people of their churches from coming to the Big Lick socials.

The socials with the work camp were even more problematic because the dances became interracial. Dark skins and light skins were intermingled. Blacks and whites of opposite sexes touched each other and swung their partners with arms and bodies intertwined as if color did not matter. It was precisely the type of social activity most feared and hated by Southern segregationists. In his journal for Friday, July 6, Smathers recorded, "We had a Social tonight with 40 present - folk acted well toward Ann" (the one African American present at the social).

AUGUST, 1945, *CALVARY FELLOWSHIP* (the parish newsletter published monthly from 1937–1947): "WAR IS OVER" was the first headline, and page 1 was devoted to reflections on the war's end and a welcome home to several servicemen and women. On the next page, Smathers reported on the work camp, writing,

> The Work Camp . . . was a new and valuable experience for us. The young people who came were all most appreciative of the hospitality and friendship shown them. I had confidence that Big Lick would give them a cordial welcome as a Christian community should, and it did, and I am proud . . . It was a mutual experience . . . for a little while we shared a Christian fellowship across barriers of difference . . . The only unpleasant experience of the six weeks occurred on the last night of the camp when four little "Hitlers" fortified with liquor went up and down the road breathing oaths and threats. The occurance [*sic*], while not so much in itself, is an indication of the problem before us and the world.

In a way, it was a blessing that Big Lick was an isolated community. Those outside of Big Lick and Calvary Church who were opposed to black folk in their midst and especially to interracial dancing did not learn what was happening for a time. Then they hardly had time to organize any opposition. Nevertheless, in his journal for Friday, August 10, 1945, Smathers was a little more forthcoming than in the church newsletter. He wrote, "Had social tonight (38 present) - a good time except for some 'smart "alecs,"' [*sic*] [of which he names four and notes two others], who cursed & threatened up & down the road. Had to call the sheriff." On Sunday August 12, he wrote, "Carl W. is still breathing 'hatred' - jumped on Fred yesterday." It was a harbinger of things to come.

"First Interracial Work Camp in the South – 1945."

Summer, 1946

Smathers, Morton, and the whole FSC executive committee were ecstatic over the success of the 1945 camp. Smathers and Morton speculated that the work camp's success demonstrated that attitudes were really changing in the South. All it had actually demonstrated was that the racial attitudes in one small exceptional Southern church were changing, and that change had not even reached past the perimeters of the community that church represented. Their euphoria would be turned to dust in the summer of 1946.

SATURDAY, JUNE 29, 1946, BIG LICK, TENNESSEE: The first members of the second interracial work camp ever held in the rural South arrived today. By July 1, all six of them will be here. There will be one African American among them, a young man named Bill Shepperd.

This work camp group joined in its first Big Lick social on July 5. In addition to the six work campers, there were thirty-four Big Lick young people in attendance. It did not go as smoothly as Smathers had hoped. In his journal for that evening, he wrote, "Some flare up of racial prejudice - which bothers me considerably."

After the service on Sunday, July 7, Smathers talked with the men of the church about the budding problem. In his journal for that date, he recorded, "Good [church] service. Talked with the men about the camp - excellent support." Nevertheless, he broke some engagements and rearranged his schedule to ensure that he would not be out of the community while the work camp was there.

The next week went smoothly enough—until Friday night. The work campers spent part of their time that week visiting in the homes of Big Lick families. One family (the Halls) even gave a party for them. The social on that Friday, July 12, 1946, began as usual about 6:30 PM. In addition to the six work campers, about thirty Big Lick young people were present. Heeding Smathers's warning of the previous Sunday, six to eight of the older men of the church were also present, most of them World War II veterans.

In a field about a half mile from the church, another group of nine to twelve men gathered at their rendezvous point that evening. Most of them were not from Big Lick proper but from neighboring communities, although some from Big Lick were also among the group. They too were heading for the church social that night, but they had another kind of dance in mind. They consumed copious amounts of beer and moonshine and waited until almost dark before they burned the cross they had brought with them. They were working up their courage for the mission that lay ahead.

Around 8:30 PM, eight couples were on the floor of the church social room following the caller through the moves of a square dance called "Red River Valley." Bill Shepperd was coupled up with a white girl from the work camp. The strains of Michael Herman's Folk Dance Band could be heard spinning an up-tempo version of "Red River

Valley" out of the old 78 rpm Victrola. The melodious voice of the caller could be heard above the music and the noise of the dancers:

> Allemande left with your corner lady
> And a grand right and left hand half way round,
> Then you swing your honey baby
> And promenade her right back home
>
> Now the Head Couple leads down the valley
> And you circle to your left and back to your right
> Now you swing the girl of your Red River Pal
> And then you swing your own Red River gal

It was about that time that the night riders arrived. They had come directly from their rendezvous place and had drunk their fill of courage. They were all on horseback. One stuck his horse's head through a window and shouted, "Where's the n——r. We want the n——r boy!" Immediately, Smathers shut down the record player and told all the dancers to stay inside the building. The older men of the church who were there quickly formed a phalanx between the horsemen and the church. There were no guns displayed, but the heavy overall pockets of these men signaled to the night riders that they meant business.

Among those who in Smathers's words "bluffed" the night riders that night were Big Red Bradley, Little Joe Selby, and three of the Hall boys. All these were recently back from the Anzio invasion, the beaches of Normandy, and central Europe. Having seen some of the worst fighting of WWII, they were not easily intimidated by a drunken mob of their fellow hillbillies. The Hall boys' father, Uncle Albert, was also present. The local store owner and postmaster, he was a little bantam rooster of a man who was perhaps the bravest of them all. Others, lost to history, may also have been present.

In his journal for that evening Smathers called the situation "very tense" and "pretty serious." But these terms severely understate the situation. This was the same type of mob, empowered by a fierce racial hatred and braced by alcohol, which had brutalized, tortured, and lynched other African Americans around the South. During that same July, in another rural Southern community, two black couples were lynched at Moore's Ford Bridge in Walton County, Georgia, about sixty miles east of Atlanta, supposedly because one of the black men, a WWII veteran, had been too friendly with white women. At the Big Lick social that July night, a black man was dancing with white women. There was no doubt among those present that had the mob gotten hold of Bill Shepperd, they would have done him harm.

What transpired between the phalanx of armed church members and the mob that night was a nose-to-nose confrontation that took place primarily between the leaders of the night riders and Gene Smathers. The mob shouted, cursed, called Bill Shepperd and Gene Smathers disparaging names, and threatened violence. They called Shepperd a "n———r," a "coon," a "black b———d," and a coward for failing to come out and face them. Face-to-face with Smathers, they called him, "A GD n———r-loving SOB" and every other vile slur and curse word that came to their minds. They threatened to "Stomp his a———" if he did not get out of their way so they could get to the "n———r boy." Smathers met this onslaught with a calm reminder that they were on church grounds and should watch their language. And he told them in no uncertain terms that they were not going to get their hands on Bill Shepperd or anyone else inside the church building. He did not flinch. After forty-five minutes or so, the night riders gave up, turned their horses, and left.

This may be the first instance ever in which members of a white Southern community put themselves in harm's way to protect the rights of an African American individual to participate in an interracial social event. But their stance did not save the camp. Two days later, Sunday, July 14, Smathers's journal records, "Didn't preach but discussed the situation re the Work Camp." On Tuesday, July 17, Smathers records, "Went to Crossville. Saw Mr. Sabine [the church's attorney]. He advised closing camp. Group decided to leave tomorrow." Sabine advised

Smathers that he could expect no help from the local sheriff and that the mob might grow stronger and more dangerous if the camp continued.

On Wednesday, July 17, Smathers wrote in his journal, "Helped group get ready to be off. Took Bill Shepperd and Harriet to bus at noon. Came back for another load . . . Took others to Crab Orchard about 4:30. They caught a ride at once . . . A fine experience (potential) ended today due to the prejudice and irrational hate of an irresponsible group."

AUGUST 1, 1946, THE *CROSSVILLE CHRONICLE*: In a letter entitled "Is This Free America?" and printed in the *Chronicle* on this date, Albert Hall briefly described the events at Big Lick on the night of July 12 and then wrote,

> On this occasion these visitors, along with the pastor of the church, were insulted and threatened in a manner sufficient to shock the imagination of any loyal American citizen . . . I sometimes wonder where we are headed. For the last four years our boys have fought and died by the thousands for what we call "liberty." Let me ask: "Is this it? . . . Is this free America?" . . . NO, not as long as American citizens are treated as this Negro boy was treated in our county or any other place in the U. S. A . . . . Are we to turn our county over to persons of prejudice and hatred? The group of Christian young people mentioned above came for a six-weeks stay . . . They were here less than three weeks . . . Let us pray for those who did this evil deed. Let us pray the prayer the Master prayed while hanging on the Cross, hanging there because of prejudice and hatred, "Father forgive them, for they know not what they do."

Smathers was heartened by Mr. Hall's letter, by the stand of the men of the church, and by a "nice letter" he received from Bill Shepperd on July 25, but he was discouraged that the racists had won the day and gotten what they wanted. In the years that followed, dozens of people of color, including some African Americans, came through Big Lick on short visits (a few hours to a couple of days), and they were always welcomed warmly by the members of Calvary Church. However, none stayed long enough to elicit opposition.

Smathers himself continued to be deeply involved in promoting racial equality and integration through the Fellowship of Southern Churchmen and otherwise. He continued to send annual membership dues to the NAACP. He served, virtually every summer, as an instructor for African American sharecropper ministers, often being the only white person in attendance at these events generally held on the campus of a historically black college. He continued to preach on race relations. However, he felt that the mob's success in forcing closure of the 1946 work camp left a black mark on Big Lick and on his ministry. He yearned for an eraser to get rid of that black mark. The opportunity would come eight years later.[3]

"Folk dancing – 1940"

Fall 1953–Summer 1954

SUNDAY, NOVEMBER 8, 1953: The Calvary Church session met today and recorded in their Minutes book: "Plans for building additional SS rooms were discussed and approved in general. Approval was given for the idea of securing a student work camp for next summer to help with the building of the SS rooms and completion of the community shop." No mention was recorded at that time that the work camp might be interracial.

SUNDAY, APRIL 25, 1954: The Calvary Church session and deacons met after church on this date and recorded the following in their minutes: "Session and Deacons met after church to discuss work camp. Mr. Smathers pointed out that the group might be interracial, and we need to be sure of our intentions before inviting group. Motion made, seconded and passed that we invite a group of students from Kalamazoo, Mich. to spend the month of August assisting us on the SS building. Plans were made to get the building underway before students arrive." The minutes are signed by A. H. Hall, clerk, and Eugene Smathers, moderator.

Although the minutes are brief and to the point, there can be little doubt that those making this decision knew their intentions and the trouble they were potentially inviting. They met in late April as *Brown v. the Board of Education* was working its way through the Supreme Court. It would be decided on May 17, 1954. Several of those at the session meeting had been present at the confrontation in 1946. A. H. Hall had written the scathing letter to the local paper after the 1946 incident. They hardly could have been more clearheaded about the direction they were taking.

WEDNESDAY, JULY 21, 1954, BIG LICK, TENNESSEE: The work campers arrived about five thirty this afternoon. Gene Smathers met with them tonight and wrote in his journal, "Nice group" and then proceeded to list their names. No special notation is made by the name Andy McCullough, but that is the name that would resonate throughout Big Lick for the next month and continues to echo in the minds of the few still living who experienced that summer.

Anderson Thoran K. McCullough ("Andy" to everyone who knew him) was a Kalamazoo College football player, 225 heavily muscled pounds on a six-foot-four frame. He would have stood out among the others in any circumstances because they looked soft and out of shape in comparison. But the thing that mattered most, what really made him stand out, was the deep ebony color of his skin.

In his journal for Sunday, August 1, Smathers recorded, "People seemed to give Andy McCullough a cordial welcome." However, everything was not as cordial on August 2, when Smathers records, "We got in a good days work on building. Y.P. did exceptionally well... I talked to camp tonight about the [Cumberland] Plateau. Local boys did a little shouting during the session."

On the evening of August 3, the work camp and local young people gathered for an informal social at the church. It was an opportunity for the local youth to get to know the work-camp group. Somewhat shyly at first, but more enthusiastically as the evening advanced, a couple of the local high school girls took turns as Andy McCullough's partner in the folk dances. Perhaps these particular girls liked to push the taboo boundaries further than most were willing to do. Perhaps it was because Andy was a little exotic, and it did not hurt that he was a lot of things that many of the local boys were not. He was handsome, polite, cultured, well educated, gentlemanly, and extraordinarily nice.

Mike Smathers recalls overhearing a conversation outside the church between two of the local boys present that evening, one of whom was interested in one of the girls who was dancing with Andy. One boy said to the other, "Why don't you go in there and tell that coon to stay away from your girlfriend?" The other replied, "I'd end up over there in that corn field [across the road]. Have you seen the muscles on that n-----r?" Though he had been only five in 1946, Mike Smathers had heard the stories, and he expected that this conversation meant trouble.

The next day and night, August 4, went smoothly as the Smatherses met with the work camp at the health center (where the work camp group was staying) to celebrate Mike's thirteenth birthday. Thursday, August 5, was Election Day.

That evening, Smathers wrote in his journal: "Loucile & I helped with election. Large vote out. Threat of trouble tonight - gathered up several of the men. Nothing happened - hope it was only a rumor. Suspense was pretty hard on morale of us all . . . We sat guard over the work camp group tonight. Earn Blaylock was made deputy sheriff."

Again, Smathers's brief journal notation seriously understates the suspense of the situation as it is remembered by others who were there. It is true that no mob materialized that night and no one showed up to threaten this work camp the way they had in 1946. But this evening was not without its drama. The polls closed at 5:00 PM. As soon as they closed, Smathers met with a small group of church leaders who were at the polling place. His words to them were blunt: "If you allow them to run this work camp off like they did the last one, I will leave Big Lick."

By dusk, a group of twenty or more men and boys (not all of whom were church members) had gathered in the health center yard to protect the work camp. Mike Smathers remembers that some of those there surprised him, for he expected them to be on the other side. He also remembers that no weapons were visible, but they were in evidence if one inspected the pockets of the men and the insides of the vehicles gathered there.

At the edge of the yard sat a black-and-tan sheriff's cruiser. The deputy in the cruiser was relaying a conversation between Sheriff Charlie Johnson in Crossville and Smathers who stood beside the cruiser surrounded by half a dozen other men and boys. The car's two-way radio squawked a message that was barely intelligible to those outside the car. The deputy interpreted, "The sheriff says you better get him [meaning Andy McCullough] out of here. We can't protect him." Smathers replied, "Tell the sheriff he is not going anywhere. We are going to keep him right here." The deputy relayed the message and got the reply, "Tell them they are on their own. We don't have any deputies to spare. We can't help them."

Smathers replied, "Tell him he needs to appoint someone out here as a deputy." The deputy relayed the message, and the two-way radio squawked again. "The sheriff says who do you want him to appoint?" relayed the deputy. Smathers conferred with the other men around him. They decided that Earn Blaylock would be the best choice. So right there over the squawk box, Earn Blaylock was sworn in as a deputy sheriff.

Blaylock was in some ways an odd choice. A retired miner and farmer, he had been a World War I naval midshipman, but he was blind in one eye and had no law-enforcement experience. The "one-eyed Jack" some of the boys called him. However, he lived almost directly across the road from the church and, being retired, was free to watch over the camp during the day. Thereafter, as the work camp worked across the road, Blaylock sat in his rocking chair on his front porch with his shotgun either on his lap or resting against the wall next to him. Others would help him with the nights.

FRIDAY, AUGUST 6, 1954, ABOUT 6:00 PM: A car pulled slowly into the driveway at the manse (home of the Smatherses). Smathers met it halfway up the driveway. Inside the car, Estille Burgess was at the wheel and Elmo "Red" Bradley was in the front passenger seat. A pistol rested beside each man. In the backseat was the "one-eyed Jack" with his shotgun between his legs. Smathers, unarmed, got in on the other side of the backseat. They and a couple of other carloads of armed men took turns sitting guard over the work camp that night and for several nights thereafter.

Nothing much ever materialized from the rumors that circulated on that Election Day though the group canceled all other socials where there might be interracial dancing. Perhaps it was merely an idle rumor, but an event on the camp's last night in Big Lick suggest that the community's armed protection had scared off any would-be attackers. On the last night of the camp, when the camp gathered for a picnic, a few carloads of rabble-rousers drove back and forth past the event, shouting obscenities and racial slurs. Andy McCullough stood at the edge of the road and dared any of those in the cars to come and face him "like a man" until some cooler heads persuaded him to desist from antagonizing drunken thugs.

Mike Smathers remembers one other slightly scary incident. An older young man from a community across the county, known to harbor racist sentiments, came through Big Lick and, upon seeing Andy, asked Mike malevolently, "You got n——rs down here!?" Mike, scared out of his gourd that the debacle of 1946 might be repeated, quickly replied, "He's only here to work for a little while." That seemed to placate the other young man.

Far more significant than what did not happen is what did. During the camp's stay in Big Lick, no fewer than five families had the work campers in their homes for meals and social events. They conducted a scavenger hunt that took them to several homes in the community. There were five Sundays when worship at Calvary Church was integrated. On their last Sunday in Big Lick, four of the work campers, including Andy McCullough, spoke movingly about their experience. There was a big crowd at church that Sunday with dinner on the grounds. When Andy finished speaking, there were several wet eyes among members of the congregation. In the Smatherses' guest book, McCullough wrote, "I will always remember Big Lick as one of my greatest experiences."

The black mark of 1946 had been erased. It had only been one short month, but Calvary Church and the people of Big Lick had demonstrated that people's common faith in Jesus Christ could be more powerful than the prejudices and intolerance that forced them apart. At least for a moment, Gene Smathers and Big Lick had shown that one of the "dividing walls of hostility" Paul wrote about in Ephesians could be broken down, even if for a short time and in one small rural Southern community.

These work camps did not change the attitudes of many white Southerners. They did not appreciably advance the cause of civil rights in the South. What they did do was demonstrate that with the right leadership, a rural white Southern community could be turned at least ninety degrees on the issue of race and that a few of the people in that community could be turned around 180 degrees on racial attitudes. That was not such a small victory in 1954.

"Third Interracial Work Camp – 1954"

NOTES

1. More about Nelle Morton's interesting life can be found in Answers.com or on the Talbot School of Theology: Christian Educators Web site (*www.talbot.edu/ce20/*. (Go to Protestant Educators and look her name up in the list).

2. Eugene Smathers, *Journal* for Sunday, March 4, 1945.

3. There is an account of these first two work camps and more about the Fellowship of Southern Churchmen (FSC) in the chapter "Flag-Bearers for Integration and Justice" - "Local Civil Rights Groups in the South 1940-1954" by John A. Salmond in the book <u>Before Brown: Civil Rights and White Backlash in the Modern South</u>, edited by Glenn Feldman (the University of Alabama Press, 2004), 222–237. Unfortunately, this work does not cover the Fellowship prior to 1940, and its account of the two work camps appears to be taken entirely from correspondence between Eugene Smathers and Nelle Morton. Mr. Salmond did not interview any of the people who were present during the camps' stays in Big Lick, nor did he have access to Gene Smathers's journals or other papers, nor access to Albert Hall's letter to the local paper. Neither does he have any information on the 1954 work camp since it was not sponsored by the FSC. Therefore, his innuendo that the Calvary Church congregation may have been partially responsible for the failure of the 1946 camp is substantially incorrect.

CHAPTER 11

THE BUZZARDS COME HOME TO ROOST

In 1957, three years after the last interracial work camp, Gene Smathers found himself caught up in the most serious "red baiting" incident of his ministry. And it was not of his own making. It began when Highlander Folk School decided to have a twenty-fifth anniversary celebration. Highlander had begun as a place of training for unionists and labor leaders. It was there that the Fellowship of Southern Churchmen was born, and Smathers had become more involved with them primarily through their common efforts to organize a Tennessee Farmers Union in the 1940s. By 1957, Highlander had switched its emphasis to the civil rights movement, but Gene Smathers remained a member of its board of directors.

Gene Smathers was not at that twenty-fifth anniversary celebration. In fact, he had almost forgotten his entanglement with Highlander. As a member of the board of directors, he was in a figurehead position. The board seldom met. Myles Horton, founder and director, ran Highlander pretty much according to his own drummer without much, if any, consultation with the board of directors. Smathers may or may not have even have been invited to that twenty-fifth anniversary celebration. But a reporter from the Georgia Commission on Education was there, gaining admission on a press pass.

The Georgia Commission on Education was established by the Georgia General Assembly on December 10, 1953, for the purpose of slowing down or stopping the integration of the schools (though its founding document nowhere mentions segregation or integration). Coming out of Highlander's twenty-fifth anniversary celebration, the Georgia Commission produced two inflammatory documents.

The first of these was a slick six-page newspaper-style smear sheet. At the top of page 1, it had a picture of blacks and whites, including Martin Luther King, Rosa Parks, Miles Horton, and others, sitting together. The headline above the picture read "MARTIN LUTHER KING at COMMUNIST Training School." The second item produced was a billboard copy of this picture and headline that was posted on billboards all over the South. The newspaper-style pamphlet had a few derogatory articles about Highlander, but was mostly filled with other pictures showing blacks and whites socializing, even dancing together.

The charge that Highlander was a Communist training school was ludicrous to those familiar with the organization. It was certainly left-wing, but it was well within the boundaries of American social thought at the time. Most of those at the twenty-fifth anniversary celebration were devout Christians. But this was the 1950s and the Joe McCarthy era. For Highlander, the Georgia Commission's little slander sheet caused the state of Tennessee to launch an investigation. The resulting trial had nothing to do with Highlander being a "Communist training school" (that would not have been illegal). Although the trial was entirely about integration, the sole charge against the school was that it had sold beer without a license (beer had been consumed, but it was in the possession of certain individuals and was never sold by Highlander). The end of the trial resulted in the revocation of Highlander's charter and the confiscation of its property and its library.

Highlander was a nationally known institution supported by many individuals and organizations. Except for the loss of their land and library (now largely housed at the University of Wisconsin), which were confiscated by the state, it was hardly touched by the Tennessee trial; it actually gained from the brief notoriety. Before the trial ended, they had chartered a new organization, the Highlander Research and Education Center, which relocated and carried on Highlander's work with little interruption. Today, Highlander is renowned for its civil rights leadership, often receiving plaudits from the same newspapers that called for its dissolution in 1957.

In Cumberland County, the impact was much smaller in scale, but more intense in impact because it fell on one man who was more entrenched and dependent upon his community than those at a place like Highlander. That man was Gene Smathers. On the third page of the slick newspaper-style smear sheet from the Georgia Commission on Education was a list of the board of directors of Highlander, including Eugene Smathers. That smear sheet showed up on the bulletin board at the Cumberland County Courthouse with the headline "Communist Training School" and Smathers's name circled in red.

For weeks, Smathers had to be careful what he said and did. Even his son, then in high school, was cautioned to watch what he said and to avoid saying anything that might be taken as favorable to the Soviet Union or which might seem overly radical. To their credit, Smathers's church, at least one other church, and several individuals came publicly to Smathers's defense with letters to the editor of the local paper. Smathers was also able to plant some members of his congregation as spies in some of the more reactionary organizations in the county to see if they planned any actions against Smathers. The apprehension was very real while it lasted.

This was not the first time nor would it be the last that Gene Smathers was accused of being a Communist or Communist sympathizer. But it was the most serious and the scariest. In time, however, the scare passed over, and the incident was forgotten by all except the Smatherses and a few racial hatemongers. The latter often had Smathers near the top of their lists of Communists, which they drew up periodically.

At the moderatorial press conference after his election in 1967, Smathers was asked if it was his interracial activities that had resulted in him being branded a Communist (a fact noted in one of his nominating speeches). "Yea," he drawled. "That and the fact that I sometimes shoot off my mouth when I shouldn't." He did occasionally speak forthrightly about his beliefs. But it was never what he said, only what he did in race relations that got him into trouble.

At that same press conference, he went on to note how dispiriting it was to have people, some of whom knew of his lifelong work for the improvement of the community, whisper behind his back, "There goes that damn Communist." He spoke of how important it was to maintain a vigorous right to free expression, saying, "Brother, I know how quickly you can be shut up."

Paradoxically, 1957 was the same year that he helped to initiate the Cumberland County Planning Group, one of his more important contributions in laying the groundwork for the future of Cumberland County.

CHAPTER 12

FARMER AND FRIEND OF THE SOIL

Farmer and Farmer-Philosopher

In her recent book, <u>Founding Gardeners</u>,[1] Andrea Wulf writes about George Washington, John Adams, Thomas Jefferson, and James Madison not as statesmen and politicians, but as farmers, gardeners, and conservationists. She argues that their love and practice of farming and gardening shaped their vision of America. It is a unique new look at America's Founding Fathers and provides insights into how their love and practice of farming and gardening influenced how they thought about themselves and the new nation they were creating. It tells, also, with somewhat clearer documentation, how their political ideals shaped or did not change their activities as farmers and gardeners. In the cases of Jefferson and Madison, and to a lesser degree, Washington, their fine words about all men being created equal did not affect their use of slaves. Washington at least freed his slaves upon his death.

Her book provides fascinating reading for one looking into Gene Smathers as a farmer, gardener, and friend of the soil because so many of Smathers's ideas about farming and gardening and about farming and democracy parallel those of these Founding Fathers. Someone has said that Smathers "made his living as a minister, but he made his life as a farmer." Like the Founding Fathers, Smathers farmed, first of all, because it was essential to the well-being of his family and the economy of the community to which he was ministering. However, his view and practice of farming went far beyond the provision of practical necessities for his family. He always saw part of its purpose as replacing drabness with beauty, scarcity with abundance.

Though Smathers lived at a time when the United States was already more than 50 percent urban, he believed, like Wulf's Founding Fathers, that an agrarian society was inherently more stable and more virtuous than an urban one. Like Adams (alone among the four Founding Fathers profiled by Wulf), Smathers was a devout Christian. He believed (as Adams probably did) that human beings had a sacred obligation to the soil—that God intended for human beings to till and tend the soil and to preserve it for future generations. Smathers was certain that those who owned the land they worked with their own hands not only made better citizens but remained closer to God. They thereby made better Christians and stronger church members, helping to preserve the rural church as a viable and vital institution.

Both Smathers and Adams (and especially their fathers) represented the small landowning class of farmers (freeholders) whom the Founding Fathers believed to be the key to the success of their experiment in self-government. Adams believed that small freeholders would remain the predominant class of people in the new United States, and Smathers worked hard to maintain and expand that class of farmers.

Of the four Founding Fathers profiled by Wulf, Adams was the only one, who, like Smathers, actually engaged in and enjoyed the drudge work of farming and gardening—gathering and spreading manure and compost, clearing fields of trees, digging out ("grubbing") stumps, hoeing crops, and harvesting hay. Abigail Adams said of her husband, "Working the soil 'keeps his Spirits in action and gives him health.' Without the digging and scything," she continued, "he 'could not endure' life in Philadelphia."[2] Loucile Smathers said of her husband,

"He would work in his study until about noon, and then he had to get out and do something [on the farm or in the garden]."[3]

In both cases, the wives were as much a part of the farming operations as their husbands. Both men were away from home a great deal, and in their absences, their wives had to carry on. With respect to Smathers in particular, it is impossible to overemphasize the contribution of Loucile. When he was trying to get her to marry him, he had written her, "I can never do my best work without you by my side, but with you I feel we can do great things." While this would prove true in almost every aspect of his ministry within the Big Lick community, nowhere was it more obvious than in their farming.

As his ministry developed, Smathers was often invited to go on speaking tours or to lecture at summer schools for ministers, and for three years in the 1940s, he taught at the Vanderbilt School of Religion three days a week in Nashville. In short, he was often gone from home, sometimes for extended periods. However, the farm chores still had to be done. There was a cow to feed and milk, hogs to feed, chickens to feed and eggs to gather, garden crops to be weeded and gathered. Moreover, she helped when he was home. Until their son Michael was old enough to help, Loucile worked in the fields as hard as any man, hoeing corn, putting up hay, "grubbing" stumps, spreading manure, and so forth.

Like Jefferson, Smathers used his farm for experiments that were conducted for the instruction of his neighbors. The first yellow corn and the first hybrid corn in Big Lick were grown by Smathers on the church farm. The first winter cover crops were grown there (and one year won a prize as the best in the county). The first contour tillage, the first use of chemical fertilizers, the first crop rotation was done there. The first purebred hogs were raised there with the offspring given to other farmers in the community. He introduced purebred cattle, and when his son was older and active in 4-H, he and his son had one of the finest and most prize-winning small herds of purebred cattle in the county.

Like Madison, he tried to rally Americans to stop destroying the soil and the forests and believed that in order for America to remain a vital nation of free and independent persons and to maintain its strong place among the nations of the world, Americans had to learn to protect their soil, forests, and natural environment. He believed that to despoil the earth was to sin against both God and your neighbor. He further believed that owner occupancy offered the best chance for preservation of the soil and the small-farm lifestyle. He was opposed to absentee ownership, sharecropping, and tenant farming.[4]

Like the four Founding Fathers noted above, Smathers's farming and gardening was more than an avocation, more than just a way to help keep his family fed, more than an example for his neighbors, more than a form of recreation. It was also about the beautification of nature for the enjoyment of human beings. Farming and gardening was also a way to express his solidarity with the folk to whom he pastored. (Just as for the Founding Fathers, it was a way of identifying with the people of the nation they were bringing to life.)

Like the Calvary Church homesteaders that would follow him, he and Loucile cleared the church farm from the forest and turned it into one of the most productive small farms in the county. The Smatherses later bought a one-hundred-acre tract of woodland, cleared it, and turned it into a productive farm.

Like Jeremiah's purchase of the field at Anathoth, it was their personal investment in the Big Lick community—an expression of their faith that Big Lick would survive and continue to thrive through the Calvary Church Homestead Project. They intended to retire there, but Gene's death prevented that. It is currently owned by their son Michael and his wife, Judy, and is still being farmed.

At the height of the activity of the Calvary Church Homestead Project, Gene farmed not only the twenty-five-acre church farm and his own one hundred acres, but also all the homestead project land that was not currently being homesteaded by a family. During these years, he was often the farm manager (and he and his family provided much of the labor) for up to four hundred acres of farm and woodlands.

Beyond the depth of even John Adams, Smathers farmed partially for the metaphysical aspects of the enterprise. In the final analysis, farming is a solitary enterprise in which the only actors are the lone individual and his or her God. Subsistence and small entrepreneurial farming imposes a strict discipline. There is always milking, feeding livestock, planting, weeding, harvesting, spreading manure, and other activities that must be done within a certain time frame.

When these activities are seen as cooperating with God's purposes that life replace death and that beauty and abundance replace ugliness and scarcity; when soil and forest conservation and reclamation are seen as a means of repentance and atonement for human destructiveness, it is easy to see how these activities become, as they did for Gene Smathers, a part of one's spiritual discipline. It becomes part of the way a person comes to understand who he/she is in relation to the ultimate ground of being (i.e., God). It turns into a way in which one's faith and trust in God are deepened. In is not unlike monks who practice gardening as part of their spiritual discipline.

Like the Founding Fathers, Gene and Loucile planted thousands of non-native trees (mostly white pines) over their farm and the burned-over, damaged woodlands of the church homestead project. In addition, they planted at least twenty-nine other varieties of non-native trees on their own farm--so many different varieties that portions of their farm became practically an arboretum. He planted trees until the last year of his life and she into her seventy-fifth year. "Planting trees for a future race" Jefferson had called it in a letter to John Adams.[5, 6]

He led Big Lick to become the certified tree farm capital of Tennessee in 1951. Big Lick farmers, under the leadership of Smathers, had developed a community-wide forestry management plan. On May 11, 1951, twenty Big Lick farmers were certified as tree farmers, constituting nearly 10 percent of all the certified tree farmers in Tennessee.[7] Smathers was asked to deliver a speech at a regional conservation meeting, addressing why he, a preacher, was also a tree farmer. He said in part:

> I was one of the first tree farmers in Cumberland County . . . In my lifetime, I will never realize any financial return from these labors . . . There may be some value in the fact that I personally shall never have any income from these trees . . . Too often we tend to measure everything in economic terms, when there is so much more to life . . . I have always liked to see things grow, and it is a continuing satisfaction to see healthy, vigorous, attractive trees replace the sickly, ugly, useless scrubs . . .
>
> First, tree farming provides a means of cooperation with the creative processes of nature - which to me are an expression of the creative forces of God. Secondly, it provides an humble way of making atonement for man's destructiveness, his thought-less and careless exploitation of natures' resources . . . Each tiny tree as it was planted became a symbol of the constant war we must wage against destruction and ugliness, an expression of basic gratitude for the wonder and wisdom of God's creation, and an act of cooperation with His continuing purpose that life and growth conquer death and decay.

By 1940, his work had led him to become an advocate for small farmers, not only in Big Lick but throughout the South. Two issues concerned him particularly. One was the destruction and wastefulness of the soil and other natural resources. The very basis of farming was slowly being eroded away. This problem had been largely solved in Big Lick by persistent education and the conservation requirements of the Calvary Church Homestead Project.

The second issue was the fact that, aided and abetted by national farm policies, small farmers were increasingly being squeezed out of the economic mainstream. Large absentee landowners and "factory farms" were increasingly taking over the farm economy. It was not what the Founding Fathers had envisioned, and it was not what Gene Smathers thought was good for the vitality, character, and continued strength of the nation.

However naive the notion was that the small-farm way of life could be maintained, it animated his actions for the latter half of his working life. He first tried to help organize small farmers and sharecroppers into a union, serving on the organizing committee of the Tennessee Farmers' Union. He soon learned that organizing independent farmers who had no other ties to one another was about like herding cats.

Some people came to call him a "missionary to the soil" or a "prophet for the soil." He preferred the term "friend"—a friend of the soil.

"Gene Smathers with purebred heifer; the first purebred stock in Big Lick – 1940"

Friends of the Soil

MARCH 22, 1940, THE PRESBYTERIAN MANSE, BIG LICK, TENNESSEE: Today, Gene Smathers called together Buck Kester, Scotty Cowen, A. L. DeJenerett, and W. W. Sikes (who along with Smathers constituted the Executive Committee of the Fellowship of

Southern Churchmen). He called them together to introduce them to his idea for an adjunct organization to more particularly and more emphatically address the issues facing small farmers and the nation. These issues had to do with the wastage of the soil and other natural resources; and, secondly, with the exploitation of tenant farmers and sharecroppers. The new organization would be a "distinctly religious movement founded upon the Lordship of God over man, the earth, and its resources." They would call their new organization "FRIENDS OF THE SOIL."

In the first years of the twenty-first-century, it would most probably be called an "eco-justice" organization. It was among the first, if not the first, to raise conservation of the soil (and other natural resources) as a Gospel issue and to link it with a demand for justice for those who worked the land. It promised to sponsor legislation that would promote its purposes. It would seek assistance from like-minded individuals and groups who were working to conserve the soil and other natural resources. It would cooperate with all public and private agencies working toward "a just rural order," defined as working to improve the health and security of people on the land.

Its underlying principle was that "those who despoil the earth stand under the judgment of God no less than those who oppress His people." It proclaimed that "bread, beauty, and brotherhood" and "soils, souls, and societies" are intrinsically bound together. Although ostensibly a subsidiary of the Fellowship of Southern Churchmen, Friends of the Soil was Gene Smathers's organization. Smathers was the moving force behind its founding, served as its first chairman, and wrote most of the literature produced by the organization. The most prominent of these were two pamphlets: *Stewards of the Soil* and *A Primer for Friends of the Soil.*

Both pamphlets cover essentially the same topics, but the *Primer* is longer and more "scholarly," has more specific suggestions about what people can do and a listing of resources to help them. It might even be called a "booklet." Both pamphlets lay out the biblical basis for concern about the soil and those who tend it. Both make the case for the church to lead in the reclamation of America's soil. Both encourage the church to influence government policy. However, it is the first and shorter of the two pamphlets that is the real call to action. Like portions of Jeremiah or the first thirty-nine chapters of Isaiah, it is almost apocalyptic in tone (e.g., "Failure in stewardship brings ruin," "The United States is rapidly being wasted," "We are at a moment of crisis in our national land use policy," "The Church must help people settle on farms.").

<u>Stewards of the Soil</u> is packed with theological and practical information and sprinkled with quotations from a wide variety of sources: an African American sharecropper mother (Louisiana Dunn Thomas), the Bible, Hugh H. Bennett and Walter A. Lowdermilk (both with the United States Soil Conservation service), Lewis Mumford, and Edwin Markham among others. And of course, it notes the Calvary Church Homestead Project, Big Lick's own experiment with land redistribution and reclamation. It also gives other examples of practical action that churches and others can take. It was a manifesto and call to action addressed to the churches, but meant to reach all who had anything to do with rural land use in the United States.

Together, the two pamphlets promoted farming methods that conserved the soil. These included organic farming (called biodynamic methods at the time); crop rotation; contour plowing; the use of manure and nitrogen-fixing plants; terraces on moderately steep cropland; and leaving steep acreage in forests or permanent pasture. It was equally insistent that the ownership of the farm operation should be in the hands of those who actually worked the land.

They decried the growth of the "factory farm," the continued practice of sharecropping, and the ownership of large tracts of farmland by absentee owners. They insisted that those who work the soil needed both livability and security on the land. They advocated changes in U.S. farm policies that would promote these purposes and place the pricing of farm produce, through cooperatives and other similar structures, more fully in the hands of the farmers who actually worked the land.

Like its parent, the Fellowship of Southern Churchmen, the Friends of the Soil was never able to attract significant funding and remained a tiny organization whose membership never reached the potential hoped for by its founders. It largely failed to change any of the USDA policies or to slow the march of American agriculture toward what it has become in the twenty-first century. However, its influence went somewhat further than the good works of those in its membership who combined environmentalism and the social Gospel.

"Friends of the Land," a secular "agroecology" organization, which later merged with the Izaak Walton League, was organized in Washington DC, ironically, on the same day as the Friends of the Soil. Of Friends of the Soil, they said the following:

> We have always felt a strong tug of sympathy toward the strivings of this ... group ... Friends of the Soil lived through actual war, the greatest and most damaging one ever fought, by sheer guts, faith, and a determined sense of dedication to a practical cause eternally sound and needed . . . Little hardships [we have had] such as rather scant funds, staff, and equipment, and travel difficulties in time of war are as nothing to what the Rev. Eugene Smathers and his associates in Friends of the Soil have welcomed ardently, in order to preserve their Society and extend their work.[8]

Smathers occasionally spoke at Friends of the Land conferences and wrote for their journal.[9]

Friends of the Soil (FOS) never formally disbanded, but like its parent organization, the Fellowship of Southern Churchmen, always strapped for funds, it pretty much ran out of steam by the late 1950s. Its philosophy lived on in such places as Clarence Jordan's Koininea Farm and similar intentional interracial farming enterprises and through the work of farmers and farm organizations that had been influenced by it and/or its publications. In addition, the USDA's Soil Conservation Service adopted one of the policy positions advocated by Friends of the

Soil when they began to actively promote soil conservation practices in every rural county in America.

Looked at from a viewpoint in the early years of the twenty-first century, Friends of the Soil may be seen in a different light. Given the push in some Christian (as well as secular) circles for more organic farming; more sustainable agricultural; more marketing and consumption of locally grown produce; more extensive conservation efforts, and more environmentally sound agricultural practices; Friends of the Soil, like its parent organization, may be seen not so much as a failure but as simply ahead of its time.

"Gene and Loucile Smathers receive their Tree Farm Certification – 1950."

NOTES

1. Andrea Wulf, *Founding Gardeners* (New York: William Heinemann and Alfred A. Knopf, 2011).
2. Ibid, Wulf, p 109.
3. I am refraining here from attempting to deal with the issue of slavery although Wulf covers it quiet extensively. Adams (as opposed to Washington, Jefferson, and Madison) abhorred it. For Gene Smathers slavery was not an issue, but he considered sharecropping, tenant farming, and absentee ownership of land as objects of scorn. Had they been contemporaries, it is not hard to believe that Adams and Smathers would have agreed about slavery or about the institutions of tenant farming and sharecropping, which supplanted it.
4. For more on sharecropping and tenant farming in the 1930s see James Agee (with Photos by Walker Evans), *Cotton Tenants Three Families* (Brooklyn and London: Melville House, 2013). This is shorter and more to the point than Agee and Evans' larger book, *Let us Now Praise Famous Men*.
5. Wulf, op. cit., 189.
6. For more on John Adams as farmer, see David McCullough, *John Adams* (New York: Simon & Schuster, 2001).
   For more on Thomas Jefferson as a farmer, see Henry Wiencek, "Master of Monticello," *Smithsonian* (October 2012), 40–49, 92–97.
7. The certified tree farm program was developed by the State Division of Forestry in conjunction with the Tennessee Valley Authority and the University of Tennessee Extension Service to improve the state forests. To be a "certified" tree farmer, a farmer had to agree to follow certain specific practices that would improve his or her forestland.
8. The Editors, *The Land, a Quarterly Magazine*, vol. 5, no. 3 (Autumn 1946), 364.
9. Ibid, *The Land, a Quarterly Magazine*, 364–368.

CHAPTER 13

A LIVING LABORATORY

JANUARY 7, 1941, BIG LICK, TENNESSEE: Today, Suen-i-Wie from Ginling College, Chengdu, Szeming, China, was the first foreign visitor to sign the Smatherses' guest book. He was the forerunner of a trickle that turned into a steady stream and then a torrent. They came alone, and they came by the busloads. They came religious, and they came secular. Some came out of curiosity, some with more than a little incredulity. Some stayed a few hours, others almost a year. Mostly they fell into three categories: (1) missionaries on furlough or in training and native church leaders from China, India, Cuba, Korea, and other Presbyterian Church outposts; (2) busloads of ordinary Christians, both clergy and laity, on tour of national mission stations; and (3) work camp groups.

They came like yellow jackets drawn to sweet apples. They came to see the place for themselves and to hear the story of Calvary Church and Big Lick from one whom many now considered a sage, if not a prophet. Gene Smathers was elated to see such visitors. They helped meet one of the goals of his ministry. As he would later write,

> Though beset by many local problems, an effort has been made not to be blinded by these so that we could not see the needs of neighbors in far-away places . . . Gratitude to God and to others [who had helped Big Lick] has been the basis,

> therefore of a continuing concern for all God's children. It was not difficult to secure the interest of the church and community for bringing a displaced family from Hungary to Big Lick, and for other projects of overseas relief.
>
> Believing that to be Christian, we need to be freed from the bondage of provincialism and prejudice, every opportunity has been taken to have visitors from other regions, from other races and lands. This has borne fruit in a growing awareness that not every brother in Christ has a white skin or speaks American English.[1]

The 1940s brought a steady stream of visitors helping to lay the foundation for the sponsorship of a refugee family as well as other overseas relief actions. They also opened a new avenue of ministry for Gene Smathers. Suddenly, he was in demand as a speaker, lecturer, guest preacher, and author of other articles. Mostly the event sponsors and periodical editors wanted him to tell the story of Calvary Church and the Big Lick community. They frequently wanted as well to hear about his theology which lay behind that story.

Sometimes they would ask him to speak or write on other topics (e.g., "How to Be a Successful Pastor," "The Life of the Church and the Call to Ministry"). Seldom did he speak or write, however, without weaving some of the Calvary Church and Big Lick story into what he said or wrote.

The demands upon his time for speaking and writing escalated after the first printing of *Stewards of the Soil* in 1944. After this, people began calling him a "missionary to the soil" or even a "prophet for the soil." He began to be sought as a speaker not only by churches and church organizations, but also by secular organizations such as the Tennessee Valley Authority (TVA), local County Agricultural Agents, local and regional USDA Soil Conservation District offices, Friends of the Land, and others. The TVA made Big Lick a demonstration community and part of Smathers's personal farm a series of forest demonstration plots.

They sought Smathers not as a preacher, but for his expertise as a soil conservationist, an agricultural educator, and a tree-farming practitioner. In addition, the late 1940s and 1950 saw Big Lick's most ambitious project of overseas relief.

The Bakos Family Experiment

According to the 2022 PBS series *"The US and the Holocaust,"* directed by Ken Burns, only 5% of U.S. citizens supported resettling "displaced persons" (i.e., war refugees) in the United States after WWII. Among that 5% were Gene Smathers and his 75 member Calvary Church of Big Lick, Presbyterian. Smathers first presented the idea to the Church Session (Board) on May 1, 1949. The only reason he had not suggested it earlier was that no decent vacant house was available in the community to house such a family, and building one would take too long. Then in April, 1949, the Homestead Project purchased a place with what Smathers called "a good house" on it.

He quickly presented the idea to his church officers. He asked them if they were willing to make the assurances that were necessary for sponsorship of a "displaced persons" family. The officers reacted more enthusiastically than Smathers expected. They knew there would be opposition because some of their neighbors (and fellow church members) were hurting and could use some help themselves. They knew the question would arise (as it did), "Why bring those foreigners over here when we have so many of our own that need help?" But several in the group agreed with the statement by one of them, "Surely we can take care of one family." The officers voted unanimously that "the Pastor [is] authorized to make the necessary assurances and arrangements."[2]

By November 1, 1949, a family had been selected for Big Lick. They were Hungarian and had originally been made homeless by American bombs when Hungary was under Nazi control. They had finally fled Hungary when the Russian Communists began to take control of that country. Their name was Bakos, and they consisted of father, mother, and three daughters aged two, six, and eight (although the advance documentation had said the oldest daughter was eleven). Approved in November 1949, it would be five months before they arrived in Big Lick on April 21, 1950.

Prior to arriving in Big Lick, the Bakos family had been homeless for six years. Eight times they were prevented from embarking for America because of illness or other reasons. Meanwhile, the Big Lick folks had been busy. They had spent a year in preparation and had decided (with no input from Smathers) not to put the family in the house Smathers had suggested (it was remote and isolated), but to house them in a small house on the T. V. Hale farm that had been made reasonably comfortable. This put them in the center of the community, within sight of the church, and on the land of one of the most respected men in the community. That would mute much of the opposition and lessen the fear for the family's safety than if they lived at a remote and isolated location.

APRIL 21, 1950: The Bakos family arrived in Big Lick today. So, the little church that had sent almost all of its able-bodied young men and several of its young women off to war did its part in helping to bind up the wounds of war. It turned out that a young man from Cumberland County (not from Big Lick) had led the bombing raid in July 1944 that had left Mrs. Bakos deaf. Nevertheless, there was no recriminations or anger from the Bakos family, only the joy that they had finally arrived in America.

In a letter addressed to "Dear Friends" dated April 25, 1950, Gene wrote of the Bakos family's arrival in Big Lick. Among other things, he wrote,

> I wish all of you who have been so helpful toward our puny efforts to provide a home for this family could have shared the experience of seeing their great joy when we took them to the humble little house we had ready for them . . . Even though they could not express their feelings in English, for they speak very little English, it was one of the most moving

experiences of my life . . . . All my ministry I have tried to serve the less fortunate folk, and this has been one of the most satisfying experiences of the years, and I pray that it may continue.

However, their stay in Big Lick would be short-lived. The family spoke no English. No one in Big Lick spoke any Hungarian. The two middle children fell right in at school and began to learn English quickly. They in turn taught their youngest sister. They tried to teach their parents without success. It proved nearly impossible for the adults to make any progress with the language. It was especially difficult for the mother because of her hearing disability. The Bakos adults never did learn English adequately.

Adjustment to rural life and employment was another problem. They were urban people, and Mr. Bakos had been a baker. He tried hard but soon learned that he did not think he could make it as a farmer. Finding paying work for him was virtually impossible. Most of this responsibility fell on Gene Smathers. He was able to provide Mr. Bakos a little work on his farm and on some of the unsold homestead project properties. The Bakoses never did make an adjustment to Big Lick and rural life. Mr. Bakos was sick with a stomach ailment much of the time—most likely from stress. They longed for a place where people spoke their language and where Mr. Bakos could find work in the trade for which he was trained—baking.

Within less than a year of their arrival in Big Lick, by October 1950, they had decided to move provided they could find a city with a community of Hungarian folk and a place where Mr. Bakos could find work. As happy as he had been to see them arrive, Gene Smathers was almost as happy to see them leave. He wrote to his family on October 15, 1950, writing in part, "The Bakos family has decided to leave us . . . If he can secure a good job and a place to live in some city where there are Hungarians, I guess that is the best thing for them to do . . . I do not know just when they will leave - until that time I have to try to keep work for him to do. This has been a pretty hard job for me, and in a way not being responsible for them will be a relief." Shortly thereafter, they moved to Pittsburgh, Pennsylvania.

Gene Smathers remained in touch with them for many years, writing them often and serving as an advisor for their adjustment to American life. Whenever his journeys took him to Pittsburgh, he would visit the Bakos family where he was always greeted with the warmest reception. Their arrival in Big Lick remained one of the most moving experiences of his and their lives.

Calvary Church was one of the smallest and probably the least prosperous church to sponsor a refugee family during this period. Again, it was one of Gene Smathers's ideas that did not end as he had originally hoped and envisioned. However, it ended better than it would have had the Bakos family tried to remain at Big Lick.

The outcome of this extension of the Calvary Church ministry could have been predicted. The Bakos family was an urban family, and its only able-bodied breadwinner was a baker. Big Lick was super rural and cut-off from the nearest town. It had no need of, nor market for a baker. Had those in charge of selecting refugees for resettlement chosen a rural family with a farmer as its breadwinner, the prospects for success at Big Lick would have been greater. Those in Big Lick who initiated the project knew that it was an experiment with no guarantee of long-term success. No other church so small and no other place so rural and isolated had attempted to resettle a "displaced person's" family. Calvary Church and Big Lick could rightly claim another first and "ahead-of-its-time" action.

Moreover, the Bakos family might never have gotten to America except for the sponsorship of Calvary Church. No one who lived through the events surrounding their arrival and departure will ever forget the experience.

NOTES

1. Eugene Smathers, "My Call From God," *The New Century Leader*, Nov. 1951.
2. The Calvary Church Session (Board) Minutes Book, minutes for meeting of May 1, 1949, 40–41 and Eugene Smathers's papers and notes.

CHAPTER 14

THE LURE OF GREENER PASTURES

TUESDAY, SEPTEMBER 16, 1947, THE MANSE, BIG LICK, TENNESSEE: Buried in the middle of Gene Smathers's journal for this date along with notations about buying a calf and attending a meeting in Crossville was the following notation: *"Had telegram from E. Graham Wilson wanting me to come to N.Y. for conf. on Mon. Sept 22 to consider headquarters position in Rural Church Unit."* He had received previous inquiries about other positions, but this was the first one that he felt compelled to consider. It put before Gene and Loucile Smathers the most momentous decision they had faced since getting married.

During their fifteen years at the Big Lick Parish, events had rolled along like a well-orchestrated campaign. He had found little time to think about anything else.

1932	- Arrival in Cumberland County
1934	- The move to Big Lick
1934	- Initiation of the Big Lick "socials" youth recreation program
1934-35	- Building of Calvary Church
1936-37	- Building, staffing, and opening of the Warren H. Wilson House of Health (the health center)

1938 — Initiation of the study clubs and organization of the Big Lick Farmers' Association;

1939-40 — Organization and initiation of the Calvary Church Homestead Project; Organization and beginning operations of the community sawmill

1941 — Beginning of the building of a house of play (a recreation center interrupted by World War II and never finished)

1942-44 — Commuting from Big Lick to Nashville three days a week from September through November (in addition to helping Loucile keep things going in the community and on the church farm, Gene taught and headed up the Department of Church and Community at the Vanderbilt School of Religion)

1945 — Hosting of the first interracial, interfaith work camp ever attempted in the rural South

1946 — Hosting of the second interracial, interfaith work camp in the rural South (this one forced to leave early by racists, much to Smathers's disappointment and chagrin)

1946 — Beginning of planning and preparation for sponsorship of a refugee family from Europe

On September 22, 1947, he had a series of meetings in New York with the national leaders of the Presbyterian Church. In his journal for that day, he noted, "All seem anxious for me to take job as Assistant Secretary. Housing is one big problem. Where would we live? Certainly would mean a reduction in standard of living for us all."

He wanted to accept the offer. There could be no higher compliment for a rural church pastor than to be called from his first and only pastorate to the highest echelons of the Presbyterian Church. Moreover, he had no real evidence that taking the job would result in a "reduction in the standard of living for us all." However, the issue of "where would we live" was of real concern, and it was not just a matter of economics.

The day he arrived home from New York, he and Loucile discussed the possibilities late into the night and "decided to send Dr. Wilson word that we were *favorably disposed* but not yet ready to say a definite yes. Need time to look around and ponder a bit." [1] On October 1, 1947, Gene wrote a long letter to his mother explaining the new job offer:

> I was called to New York a little over a week ago to discover that the Board wants me to accept a position at headquarters as assistant secretary in the Rural Church Unit. This offer and its consequent decision has put us in a state of confusion. There are so many ties that bind us here in Big Lick and the whole task of making a change after fifteen years in one spot makes it hard to decide what to do. We have been trying to find God's will for us in this and to weigh all sides before we make a final decision. If I accept it will be necessary for us to move somewhere near New York and one of the greatest problems confronting us is the matter of a suitable place to live. We do not want to have to live in a city, as we would feel like we were in jail. But it is very difficult to find a place to live anywhere now, and we will have to have a place with at least three bedrooms. Our salary would be raised to $375.00 a month [three times what he was currently getting] but actually we will not make any more, if as much as, we are making here. We would have to pay rent, and clothes, food and other expenses, except for the car, would be more. This job would mean that I would have to be away from home about half the time. This is the hardest decision we have had to make and I hope we are guided aright. *Our mind at the moment is to accept*, providing we can find someone to take our place here and can find somewhere to live . . . *The leaders in the Board are very anxious for me to accept this place. They say I am their first choice and that it will give me a great opportunity for real service to the church and rural people.* All the work in the Southern mountains would be one of my major responsibilities, so I would still be in contact with Big Lick and Cumberland Mt. Presbytery. We have to make our

final decision within the next couple of weeks or so, and I will be glad when it is made, for do not do much sleeping for pondering over matters one way or another . . . If we go, our hope is that before too long we will be able to find a place in the country, near enough for me to get to New York each day, where we can have a garden and chickens at least.

Loucile was particularly excited for Gene. She had long thought he deserved a more prestigious position, and one that was less demanding (on her as well as on him). In a note to his mother, she expressed her thoughts that even if Gene did not stay in the headquarters position, he would be able to find a "nice seminary position." In fact, Loucile doubted that he would ever leave the Presbyterian headquarters if they once got there because "the cream always rises to the top," and she believed that Gene was among the cream.

Throughout the month of October, they pondered whether to stay or to go. Through friends in New Jersey, they sought information on housing and small farms for sale or rent. They compared budgets for the two locations. They prayed over their decision, seeking God's guidance, and they talked often between themselves about the decision they had to make. They investigated who (or at least what type of person) could be recruited to replace Gene as pastor at Big Lick. Gene thought about those with whom he had stood for racial and economic justice in the South. Would they view his leaving as a betrayal?

They shared their dilemma with very few of their friends and parishioners in Big Lick. One with whom they did expressed his desire that they stay, but said to them, "If the tall steeple boys up in New York want you, they must think you can do more good there than here. Maybe you could do there for the whole country what you have done here for us."

They finally made their decision on Friday, October 24, 1947. In his journal notations for that date, again mixed in with records of more mundane events of the day, he wrote, "We made the decision to stay at Big Lick this afternoon, unless the Coronet article - which is pretty bad - drives us out." He later called the _Coronet_ article, "badly over done."² The article he referred to, written by Carol Hughes, was entitled "The Little Shepherd of Big Lick" and published in the November 1947 issue (vol. 23, no. 1) of _Coronet_ magazine. Reading the article today (2014), one finds it well written, generally accurate, and very complimentary of Gene Smathers. However, it was a little too praiseworthy of Gene Smathers for his comfort (making it appear as if he had done everything by himself), and it contains three questionable quotes supposedly from local individuals that might have insulted Big Lick residents by making them seem a little more backward than they really were. The fact that Gene Smathers would consider that this article might get him "driven out" of Big Lick reveals more about him and his sensitivity to the people among whom he ministered than it does about the article.

On October 30, 1947, the mailman found dozens of outgoing envelopes in the Smatherses' mailbox. They were addressed to people all over the country, but heavily weighed toward the Northeast and the South. It was not unusual for Gene Smathers to send out several pieces of mail on any given day, but this was unusual. It was like the Smatherses' post-Christmas letter that sometimes went out to hundreds of people. Though the mailman would not peek and would never know what was in those envelopes, each one contained a copy of the following letter:

> Big Lick, Tenn.
> October 29, 1947
>
> Dear Friends:
>
> I hope each of you will excuse this joint letter which I am using as a means of informing you of our final decision in regard to the acceptance of the position as assistant secretary of the Rural Church Unit of the Board of National Missions. Each of you have shown an interest in this matter and in one way or another have been helpful to us during the weeks when we were trying to determine what God's will for us

was, and I take this means of expressing to you our deep gratitude and to let you know our decision.

After these weeks of prayerful consideration and no little tension, trying to weigh the matter from every possible angle, seeing both the new opportunities which would be ours in the offered position and the losses which would be ours by leaving a work to which we have given fifteen years, we have decided to remain at Big Lick. This decision is largely based upon the following considerations:

1. That my calling is that of the rural pastoral ministry, of working with ordinary rural folk in intimate and every-day contacts, being an active participant in normal rural community life, identified with the problems and possibilities of rural life. It is, I believe, here that I can best serve the Cause of Christ.

2. Since the above seems my Christian calling, I believe that I can best fulfill this calling here in Big Lick, seeking, with God's guidance and help, to carry forward the effort to develop a Christian rural community. This belief that our work here is not yet finished is based upon the expression of the Big Lick people, who in a meeting held in my absence, expressed an earnest desire that we remain. There were 113 people at this meeting, almost every family represented. Several friends from outside the community, including some of you to whom this letter comes, expressed a similar judgment.

3. My inability to find anyone to succeed me as pastor here who seemed to have the interest and ability to carry forward the projects for which we as a Church have a moral obligation.

4. The feeling that we Southerners who have gained some small measure of influence for the development of a more Christian South should not leave the South.

5. The difficulties confronting us in the transplanting of our family in this time of inflation, including our financial inability to secure the kind of location which we would desire as a family.

6. The fact that the new position would require me to be away from home about half of the time at the very time when our son needs to see his father occasionally, and also that my physical reaction to travel is not conducive to my best work, were minor considerations.

After much thought about the "larger" opportunities which the national position would give, I am convinced that my contribution to the Christian movement in rural life can be as great from this local base as from a New York office, although in different ways. I deeply appreciated the confidence of the officers of the Board of National Missions, and trust that by continued effort to do a constructive job here this confidence will not be betrayed. And again to you, who have been so kind and helpful in this very trying time, comes our thanks.

Sincerely Yours
Gene
Eugene Smathers

The letter speaks clearly of Gene Smathers's sense of call and his fidelity to that calling. It addresses his sense of himself as a Southerner and of his solidarity with those who were working for racial and economic justice in the South. Finally, it addresses the needs of his family that he (and Loucile) thinks can best be met by staying at Big Lick.

Twenty years later, when Gene was elected moderator of the general assembly of the United Presbyterian Church, it should have come as no surprise that he insisted on establishing the office of moderator at Big Lick. He had an office in New York, but he was seldom there. When he wasn't traveling, he was in the moderator's office in Big Lick; and if anyone wanted to reach the moderator, that is where they had to direct their letters and calls.

The India Opportunity

Almost exactly one year after the invitation to join the national staff, Gene Smathers got another communication from Presbyterian headquarters. This time it came from the Board of Foreign Missions, and it was indeed an invitation to a field of larger service. Again, the historical record begins in Gene Smathers's journal. On Friday, October 15, 1948, Smathers recorded his activities for that day, including the fact that he and his children had attended a (high school) football game, and that when they got home, they discovered that his mother and brother and family had stopped in for an unannounced visit (one of only two times that his mother ever visited Big Lick). At the end of the day's notes, almost as if it were an afterthought, he wrote, "Had letter from Art Mosher [3] wanting us to go to India for 3 years. So we have another major decision to make."

Gene Smathers was more interested in this opportunity than he had been by the invitation to join the national staff. He was to be sent as an agricultural missionary. He would be stationed in Hyderabad, but his work would be out in the field, with and among Indian farmers. He would be charged with helping people of the land improve their economic and social circumstances. He had been there and done that, and he would welcome the opportunity to try some of the things that had worked so well in Big Lick in another place, another country, another culture. He was challenged by the new possibilities, and he had always been energized by new challenges. There were, however, serious impediments to his acceptance of such a call.

First of all, Loucile was not so enthusiastic. She had followed him from Berryville to Big Lick and had been willing to go to New York. She was not so sure she wanted to go to Hyderabad, India. Chief among her concerns were these:

1. Her sister, Ruth, a semi-invalid who now made her home with the Smatherses, had no other close living relatives. Where would she go to live? What would happen to her?
2. Their daughter Pat was only fifteen and had never lived outside of Big Lick. Since there was no high school for missionary or expatriate children in or near Hyderabad, Pat would have to go to a boarding high school some distance from her parents.
3. Her own health because she suffered from serious stomach problems that might be exacerbated by the food of a foreign culture.

They struggled with the decision for several weeks, but soon realized that the impediments were too great. Some of the reasons were the same as they had given for rejecting the national staff position, but in the end, it was primarily these family considerations that led them to reject the offer. Gene did so with some regret, but took solace in the belief that perhaps the Hand of God had been involved in this decision. Perhaps Big Lick was where God wanted him to be.

NOTES

1. Smathers, Eugene, Journal entry (Sept. 23, 1947).
2. Eugene Smathers, letter to J. Carson Prichard, June 27, 1951.
3. Art Mosher was principal of the Allahabad Agricultural Institute (the principal Presbyterian agricultural mission in India).

CHAPTER 15

"GREAT DAY IN THE MORNING"

Big Lick, Tennessee is not a county, or a city or a town. It is just a place. Greyhound bus drivers in Crossville, 14 miles away, have never heard of it. The 50-odd families in Big Lick carved their little farms out of the rolling, wooded country of the Cumberland Plateau. Timber used to be their cash crop. When the timber market went bad, there was nothing left but hard scrabble farming.

The average family's cash income at Big Lick was $50 a year. For six months a year even the road to Crossville was impassable. By the time a doctor was sent for, it was usually too late. When a visiting preacher came to Big Lick, he used the schoolhouse.

This was the place and these the people among whom Pastor Eugene Smathers came with his young wife to live and work and serve God.

Gene Smathers is a farmer himself - and a good one. He is a tall, stoop-shouldered, humble man with an engaging grin, a sense of humor as strong as his religious convictions – and an unharnessed imagination.[1]

Thus began the third or fourth story line for a planned Hollywood movie about the Smatherses and Big Lick. The effort went on for four years. It began in November 1946, when John Clarke Rose, a Hollywood insider, writer, and producer, visited Big Lick. It is no longer known why he came to Big Lick, nor exactly how well he was connected to the movie industry. Based on the correspondence with Gene Smathers, he seemed to have known personally Darryl Zanuck, Samuel Goldwyn, Frank Capra, Jimmy Stewart, Henry Fonda, many other actors, scores of scriptwriters, and some of the top echelon in all the major studios in Hollywood.

Rose sent the first "story line" (the first step in developing a working script) to Smathers on December 19, 1946. It was filled with feuding families, moonshiners, and a soothsaying widow who claims Big Lick is "a godforsaken place." She kept the whole community bound to outdated traditions for fear of change. The Smatherses did not get around to reading it until Christmas Day 1946. Then after opening their packages, they sat down and read the story line aloud as a family group: Gene, Loucile, Pat (age thirteen), and Mike (age five).

Based on the three-page letter Gene wrote later that day, the family did not take kindly to Rose's story line. Among other things, that letter said,

> Our reaction is a family group reaction and it is not too favorable . . . What I have hoped that the picture might do would be a portrayal of certain inherent values of rural life and how they have been deepened and strengthened by bringing the Christian faith to bear upon them . . .
>
> In you[r] treatment certain mountain stereotypes are too much in evidence, stereotypes which are so easily over worked in any presentation of this region. This approach lacks originality and immediately creates a sense of superiority and of paternalism in the mind of the outsider. We do not want to be pitied or petted, but to have the values of our way of life honestly recognized . . . What I have hoped is that your creation might do for our region what "Our Vines Have Tender Grapes" did for the region

> it portrays [Wisconsin farm country]. This was a simple, honest portrayal of the lives of ordinary rural folk, without exploitation or paternalism. This type of treatment appeals to me much more than the Jesse Stuart type of thing . . .
>
> We want a picture mountain folk can see and not feel ashamed but proud that they are as they are. *This to me is the ultimate test."* (emphasis added)

The letter continued and generally took Rose's story line apart scene by scene with specific suggestions of some things that were simply incorrect or unacceptable. They did not even like the title. Rose had suggested four alternate titles of which they liked best: "'Here Comes Tomorrow,' but fear that it has been preempted by a cooperative documentary of a few years ago. Pat suggests 'Nothing Good Comes Easy.' 'Getting Along' also had its appeal." They did not mention "Great Day in the Mornin'," which was another of Rose's suggestions and the one finally adopted. The dropping of the *g* on *morning* was probably too stereotypical for the Smatherses. The title of the final story line included the *g* although *morning* is spelled without the *g* at other places in that script.

Near the end of this comprehensive letter, Smathers wrote,

> But if this creation is worth doing, it is worth making truly worthwhile, not just another exploitation of mountain folk and their super-rural customs. We believe you have 'a big idea,' but we are not going to give our approval to any half-baked presentation of it, but want to do all we can to help you bring your own "brain-child" to more perfect fruition.

Smathers then forthrightly suggests five authors who would be good scriptwriters for the proposed movie and five books or movies that would be good examples to use in developing a story line. The letter ends on a friendly note, but what is surprising is that Gene Smathers knew as much about scriptwriting and making movies as he apparently did. Also, Smathers suggests fictionalizing the whole story and not using either the Smathers name or the actual name of the community, Big Lick. Loucile, in particular, did not like the way she was portrayed in the story line.

Rose sent a second story line to the Smatherses, but it did not get much better reception from them than the original. In response to this revision, Gene Smathers wrote to Rose on January 2, 1947: "I think your revised copy is greatly improved, but in the main my chief criticism, based upon the over use of 'mountain stereotypes' remains . . . In regard to details, few of our criticisms of Dec. 25 have been corrected in the revised pages. And I would like to make these additional suggestions." Smathers goes on to write substantial suggested revisions of five scenes in the story line. One of the things that Smathers liked was the inclusion of the story of Josiah and the felling of the walls of Jericho because, Smathers wrote, "the essential story of Big Lick was the breaking down of walls of despair, defeatism, and [outmoded] tradition."

Gene and Loucile Smathers had signed an agreement with Rose on October 31, 1946. Most importantly for the Smatherses, it afforded them veto power over the whole enterprise by including the following: "The basic story outline and treatment to meet with your personal approval." This gave the Smatherses effective control over the content of any "motion picture, radio program, play, novel, television program or similar creative enterprise produced pursuant to this agreement." Nothing having been produced as of October 24, 1949, the Smatherses signed an extension of this agreement for one year until October 31, 1950.

Rose worked hard in his effort to get a movie produced. He not only contacted all major Hollywood studios, but also several screenwriters and Jimmy Stewart, whom he wanted to fill the part of Gene Smathers in the movie. He met personally with all these, including Stewart. He used Mary Sheibley of the Presbyterian Church (who apparently knew Stewart personally), Stewart's pastor, and the pastor of the prestigious Hollywood Presbyterian Church (Stewart was a Presbyterian) in his effort to get Stewart committed to the movie. At one point, he thought he had Stewart firmly committed. There were plans for Smathers and Stewart to meet in New York City, and when that did not work out, plans were made for Stewart to visit Big Lick (that never happened either). As it turned out, Stewart was the key, and he was not as firmly committed to the movie as Rose thought.

Rose and Smathers never did reach an agreement on the basic story line although they did agree to fictionalize the whole movie and not use the Smathers name or Big Lick, or any other real name in the movie. This ameliorated Smathers's concerns some, but did not eliminate them. Smathers wanted something like the *Andy Griffith Show* but kept getting scripts more like the *Beverly Hillbillies*. He wanted a movie like *Our Vines Have Tender Grapes*; the studios wanted something like *Stars in My Crown* (a western in which the new preacher in town shoots his way to success, a movie actually made in 1950).

Moreover, in the three years (1946–1949) that Rose tried to get the Big Lick movie made, Hollywood produced three other movies about rural or small-town ministers. While totally fictional, these movies had similar themes to the Big Lick movie. In spite of Rose's continued insistence that all the necessary players were interested in making the movie, he finally admitted in 1949 that there was limited interest in producing a fourth movie with a similar theme. In addition, Big Lick was too rural. The studios wanted the story recast in a small town. The Smatherses would have none of that.

The original story line had two dramatic climaxes. The first was the confrontation over the African American young man in the second work camp. Rose and Smathers could never agree on the details of this scene. Smathers thought it was sufficiently dramatic as it actually happened. Rose wanted a mob with rifles, pitchforks, and clubs. It would not have mattered anyway for the racial issue was a subject that no Hollywood studio would have touched in 1946. The second climax was the dedication of the church, and the studios considered that too weak as a dramatic climax to carry a movie.

When he was unable to get any real movement by 1949, he extended the contract with the Smatherses and had a new story line written by someone other than himself. This is the story line that is quoted at the first part of this chapter. It had only one dramatic climax, the arrival of the displaced persons family. It apparently fared no better than the first one. In the end, it came down to the fact that no studio was willing to put up the money for a scriptwriter *unless* Jimmy Stewart was firmly committed to making the movie. Stewart was unwilling to make a firm commitment until and unless he could see and study a "shooting script." None of the studios were willing to advance the money necessary to develop such a "shooting script" without a commitment from Stewart.

The last extant correspondence on the subject is from Rose, dated March 6, 1950. At that point, Rose was still trying to get money for a screenwriter to visit Big Lick and write a shooting script. However, as early as July 25, 1947, Smathers had written to Rose: "I believe, if I were you, I would soon look for more fertile pastures unless the prospects for 'Great Day in the Morning' dawning soon does not materialize." It turned out that Smathers had a better sense of what Hollywood would do than did Rose. And that is pretty much how the affair died with the end of the contract renewal on October 31, 1950.

NOTES

[1] Louise Randall Pierson, "Great Day in the Morning" movie story line, written February 20, 1950.

CHAPTER 16

THE CUMBERLAND COUNTY PLANNING GROUP

Gene Smathers faced a dilemma. His rejection of the national staff position in 1947 and of the offer to go to India in 1948 meant that he expected to spend the remainder of his ministry in Big Lick. But Big Lick was no longer the isolated place it had been in 1934, and Gene Smathers recognized, earlier than most others, that Big Lick could no longer maintain itself as a self-sufficient rural community. Tiny farms, such as those owned by most Big Lick farmers, were becoming increasingly nonviable economically. The welfare of Big Lick families was increasingly bound together with the whole of Cumberland County.

Many of the young people who had gone off to war did not return to Big Lick—not because they were killed or wounded, but because they had seen economic opportunity elsewhere. The returning and oncoming generations of young people had little interest in finishing the "House of Play" they had begun before the war. They got no further than the foundation when the war came along, and they were unable to get materials they needed to finish it. After the war, there seemed little interest, and it never was finished.

Although the Farmers' Association, the community sawmill, the health center, and especially the Calvary Church Homestead Project were still functioning, all except the homestead project were on wobbly legs. There would be new cooperative efforts with charcoal, strawberries, and bell peppers. However, the failure of these three undertakings brought home quickly the fact that such community-based efforts could no longer sustain Big Lick families.

Roads had improved, and more people had a car or truck. Plans were already afoot to hard-surface the road through Big Lick. Highway U.S. 127 running right through the heart of Big Lick and Cumberland County was in the planning stages. Smathers himself was heading up the effort to acquire the right-of-way through Big Lick. Although it would be ten years before these roads were built, by 1960, all of Big Lick was served by all-weather roads leading into Crossville. Improved transportation brought new opportunities but also imposed new threats.

Smathers's first response was to get personally involved in a number of countywide organizations. In the late 1940s, he joined the Uplands Hospital Board and the ongoing efforts of Dr. May Wharton and Dr. Robert Metcalfe to establish a hospital in Crossville. By 1950, they had established a hospital in Crossville to serve the whole county. The little Big Lick health program that had been so influential in attracting Dr. Metcalfe to Cumberland County would soon cease to exist, but in dying, it had helped to give birth to better health services for the whole county.

Smathers helped organize the countywide Cumberland Farmers' Cooperative and served on its board almost continually until his election as moderator of the general assembly of his church. He was serving as chairman of the local farmers' coop board when he was elected moderator, and it is believed that he is the only person to ever simultaneously hold both of these positions. However, he soon relinquished the coop chair to Elmo "Red" Bradley, a Big Lick farmer who had learned the principles of cooperatives through the Big Lick study clubs and Farmers' Association.

Smathers also joined the county library board where as treasurer he became their chief spokesman in efforts to get funding from the county court. He became a member of the United Fund Board, the County

Health and Welfare Committee, the Mental Health Association, the Hull-York Lakeland Resource Conservation and Development Board. He continued to serve on these and other countywide organizations until his election as moderator of his denomination.

A major consideration of his move into countywide organizations and activities was that he did not go alone. At least a dozen of his parishioners followed him into leadership positions in countywide organizations. Having learned and developed their leadership skills in the Big Lick endeavors, having learned that people could organize to solve their own problems, they moved easily into countywide positions. So evident were Big Lick people in countywide leadership positions that in the 1950s, it was rumored that there was not a single countywide organization without someone from Big Lick in a leadership position.

This had to be satisfying to Gene Smathers. Two of his primary goals as a community developer were the development of indigenous leadership and helping people of the community assume responsibility for some of their own problems. Instead of doing everything for them, he taught and led them to do things for themselves. This was the importance of the Big Lick folk building the church (and later the health center) themselves. Having learned on these two projects (both greatly desired in the community) that with a little help they could get together and accomplish great things (even things they had previously thought impossible), they were willing and ready to tackle other endeavors.

It was not long, however, until Smathers recognized that there were too many organizations with too little communication and too little coordination among them. Smathers and another Big Lick native and resident, Roy Hall, spent long hours in Smathers's study discussing what could be done about this problem. Hall sort of became Smathers's protégé with respect to community development.

When Hall said, "Gene Smathers did not think like other men,"[1] he was referring to Smathers's uncanny ability to see the future more clearly than most and to devise instruments for dealing with the problems that future presented. The idea for an overall countywide planning and leadership group grew out of discussions between Smathers and Hall during the fall and winter of 1956. Hall was a great promoter and salesman, but he was not an organizer. Smathers was. So Smathers drew up a plan for such a group.

By February 1957, Smathers and Hall had contacted virtually every person that was in a leadership position in any organization in the county. They called a meeting for February 2, 1957, to present Smathers's plan and hopefully to organize a "Cumberland County Planning Group." According to notes in Smathers's journal for that date, they met from "9:30 am until 2:30 pm" and the group that met was a "good representation and [gave] a fair response to the idea."

In fact, they formally organized themselves into the "Cumberland County Planning Group," adopted, with some modifications, the purposes, principles, and guidelines drafted by Smathers and elected an executive committee that according to Smathers's presentation was "the key to the success of the whole plan." It would be the action arm of the group. It was essential, they agreed with Smathers, that "this Committee be composed of representative people who are willing to devote much thought, time, and effort to the development of the whole county." The whole planning group would meet twice yearly, but the executive committee would meet monthly (or perhaps more often) and would act to fulfill the purposes of the planning group. Among those elected to the executive committee were Roy Hall as vice chairman and Eugene Smathers. Also elected was Ethel Metcalfe, wife of Dr. Robert Metcalfe.

According to Smathers's plan, their "overall purpose" was "the fullest possible development of Cumberland County for the achievement of a better living for all the people." Their objectives included the following:

1. To provide some simple workable plan by which the work of the many public agencies, civic groups, organizations and citizens committees may be coordinated for realization of this over-all purpose for a better Cumberland County. A way by which these agencies and voluntary groups may pool their thought

and effort in the choice of long-term goals for over-all county development . . .
2. [To seek] greater cooperation between town and county, between the various voluntary groups and organizations, between the people and their tax-supported public agencies, and between the various agencies themselves.
3. To present a united front in confronting governmental bodies with needs and with programs contributing to total county development.
4. To discover areas of need or specific problems about which little or nothing is being done, and to encourage one or more of the existing agencies or organizations to give these some attention.

They were to be "an entirely voluntary, advisory group - taking no action itself - but seeking to coordinate and stimulate the action of existing groups and organizations." They were "not to be a pressure group but will seek to win support for over-all goals and objectives simply on their merit." They would seek participation from the "widest possible representation of every interest in the County." They would meet twice a year to discuss the "problems, needs, and resources of Cumberland County"; to project goals for the overall development of the county; to offer encouragement to and hear reports from participating agencies and organizations; and to "explore areas of need in which no present organization is working."

They set a second meeting for April 2, 1957. At that meeting, they would ask representatives of "each organization to present the goals of their organization for 1957" and to "indicate at what point its program contributes" to the overall development of the county. There were at least nineteen people representing at least fifteen different organizations present at the second meeting on April 2, 1957. At least half of these groups gave extensive reports outlining their goals for 1957.

The executive committee immediately set another meeting for the following week. At that meeting on April 9, 1957, the executive committee began laying plans for their work together. They set another meeting for the next month, May 6, 1957. Few, if any, other records exist documenting the details of what the Cumberland County Planning Group did over the next three years. What is known is that the group, or more precisely its executive committee, continued to meet regularly from 1957 to 1961. Their work met with some success and laid the groundwork for much of what was to come later. They were able to attract a small factory to locate in Crossville and improved the climate for other factories to follow. In 1961, the Cumberland County Planning Group morphed itself into the Cumberland County Chamber of Commerce with Ed Donnelly as president and Roy Hall as executive secretary.[2]

NOTES

[1] Roy Hall to Mike Smathers, conversation, August, 1968.
[2] Information taken from the papers, notes, and journals of Eugene Smathers. As far as is known, no other records about the organization and activities of the Cumberland County Planning Group exist outside the papers and records of Gene Smathers.

CHAPTER 17

SINNERS IN THE HANDS OF A LOVING GOD

The Gospel According to Gene Smathers— The Centrality of Love and Community

PORTLAND, OREGON, MAY 19, 1967: At the news conference following the election of Eugene Smathers as moderator of the 179th General Assembly of the United Presbyterian Church USA, one of the reporters asked, "What is your approach to evangelism?" "Well," Smathers first drawled in his jocular, self-effacing way, "my approach hasn't worked very well. My churches are the same size as when I went there thirty-five years ago."[1] The reporters laughed. Then in a more serious tone, he said, "No, I believe you win people by loving them. You've got to be with people and show the love of God through our love for them."

In a 1949 lecture, he said of evangelism:

> The primary task of the Church and the basic function of the minister is evangelistic: winning men [sic] to Christ. His Gospel must become vitally effective in all the relationships of life. We must not confuse evangelistic purpose with evangelistic method. The purpose may permeate many activities which would not be called evangelistic. This

> evangelistic purpose means building of Christian community beginning with the local neighborhood and extending in ever widening circles to include the whole of mankind. This [building of Christian community] is . . . the practical expression of the evangelistic purpose of the Church. It is also our most effective evangelistic method. "By this shall all men know that ye are my disciples, if you have love for one another." *Love means community.*[2] (emphasis added)

Love was one of the core "convictions" that buttressed his belief system. Six years earlier, he had spoken more extensively about his "convictions" and their relationship to the centerpiece of his theology—the creation of Christian community. There he had said,

> Through all these years, a few basic Christian convictions have motivated our efforts, convictions that have deepened as we have tried to relate the Gospel of Jesus Christ in all its fullness and with all its implications to the whole of life [in this small community]:
>
> 1. *The unity of life* within the sovereign will and redemptive purpose of God. There can be no division between body and soul, sacred and secular, spiritual and material. They are all bound together in an indissoluble unity. Our task as Christians is to strive to bring *all* people and *all* areas of life into subjection to Christ and His love. God is sovereign of all areas of human life or He is sovereign of none. Jesus is Lord of all of life or He is Lord of none of it.
>
> 2. *Love is the law of life* . . . And love can be realized only in a community of life, in responsive and loving relationships . . . *Our goal, always beyond our grasp, has been the establishment of a Christian community* . . . a community characterized by love in all its manifold relationships: love of God, love of man, love of soil . . . [A community in which] each [person] will seek the welfare

>   of all, and all will seek the welfare of each . . . [And in which] the law of love will find expression through cooperation in all areas of the community's life.
>
> 3. *The Church as the servant people of its Servant Lord must engage the world* - "as my Father has sent me, even so send I you." It is not in retreat from the world. It does not exist for itself but as the Body of Christ, the salt, the leaven, must minister to all within its reach in the wholeness of their lives . . .

The Church cannot escape involvement in changing community life, for it is called to be God's Servant People, a 'Colony of Heaven,' in the real world where the decisions of life are made. This is because God makes Himself known in real history, and His will and purpose have to do with real history, the place where life is lived. He has placed us in communities and given us work to do . . .

Jesus teaches us to pray for 'our daily bread' because daily bread is important, the ways we get it are important, that all have enough is important.

All this relates to community: to its economic arrangements and social relationships, to its stewardship of natural and human resources, to its sense of justice and fair-play, to its scale of values and ideals. *How people live together is a Christian concern*. The Christian life is a life of the Spirit which moves within the changing structures and relationships of the community - criticizing, attacking, constructing, revising, experimenting, co-operating - as God gives light and as means are available. *It is a life of love which always confesses its own involvement in the problems and pains of community life and accepts exposure and risk for [the community's] redemption.*[3]

The relationship between church and community became one of his specialties. In October 1941, in another paper/article, he expanded upon his theology of church and community:

> The church should be the unifying center of the whole life of the community . . . The emphasis of the church . . . will not be the aggrandizement of the church as an institution; [but] upon the building up of the whole community in love . . . the church exists not for itself but to bring the holy and loving purposes of God to bear upon all the relationships and affairs of the community . . . It is my faith that . . . the rural church itself will grow in proportion to the degree in which it loses itself in service to its community . . . the church as the "serving" center of the community is the keystone [to making] religion effective in all of life.
>
> There will be a recognition of the unity of body and soul . . . The common contrasts between sacred and secular, between spiritual and material, will disappear in the inclusive truth that every aspect of life needs to be responsive to the sovereign will of God . . . No vital human interest or concern will be foreign to the province . . . of the rural church . . . The greatest concern and effort will be for the marginal members, recognizing that . . . a community is no stronger than its weakest family . . . Not merely individual religious living, but all the concerns of community living have a place in our services of worship . . .
>
> If the Gospel has implications for every aspect of life, then we must not seek to win persons to it under false pretenses, but must boldly proclaim that the call of Christ is a call to His way of life, a call to contribute to the building of a Christian community.

Quoting Dr. J. H. Oldham, he continued, "The church should be a place where barriers of race, nationality, class, sex, and education are done away with, where the under-privileged, the down-trodden, the outcast and despised, find a welcome . . . a society the members of which bear one another's burdens and seek the good of all.

"The program of the church," he went on, "should help the community become a cooperative enterprise in which each individual and family has a stake . . . and when I say that the church program . . . will be concerned with every need of its community, I mean that quite literally – a concern not merely for what we call 'spiritual needs,' but for all the needs of the people."

He then goes on to briefly outline areas in which the church should be active: "Health . . ., recreation . . ., economic life . . ., education . . ., encouragement of cooperatives . . ., opportunity for youth . . ., stewardship of soil and natural resources . . ., stewardship of personal abilities . . ., and stewardship of time."[4]

Earlier that same year, he had written, "The . . . community will be characterized by love in all its manifest relationships: love of God, love of man, love of soil. The spirit of neighborliness and cooperation will be manifest in every aspect of its life . . . High standards of honesty, integrity, thrift, kindness and service will prevail." He then lists some impediments to the creation of a Christian rural community: "Defeatism, self-satisfaction and satisfaction with present conditions, an individualism which hinders or prevents cooperation, a tenacity of tradition and custom . . . and a sort of 'know-it-allness' [*sic*] that discredits the aid of experts and resists new ideas."[5] Then he lights into the impediment that most troubled him:

> A sentimental religion divorced from life . . . many professing Christians who can see no relationship between their religion and health, or play, or economic development . . . the primary aim is to get to heaven and avoid hell. Such religion finds its expression, not in a way of life, but in an annual emotional spree at the revival. Tremendous power is generated but is hitched to no constructive end . . .

> The ease of this religion makes distasteful a religion of demands. This other-worldly conception of religion is largely responsible for many other factors which hinder the development of a Christian community.[6]

Such "sentimental religion" was a lifelong antagonist to his understanding of the Gospel. He often recalled how as a child he had heard preachers who were "too much interested in damnation and too little concerned with Grace." They preached sermons, he said, "that rivaled Jonathan Edwards's *Sinners in the Hands of an Angry God*." He recalled nightmares of people standing above a burning abyss with nowhere else to go like ants on the end of a burning log in a brushfire.

By the time he was in high school, he had decided that this was not the kind of God or Gospel in which he believed. He wrote in 1951, "[Unlike Moses], I had no burning bush; but a fire burned within, creating a compelling desire to serve Christ by serving rural people, using whatever talents and skills God had given me *to lead them out of social and spiritual bondage into the freedom and fullness of the Gospel of God's kingdom*"[7] (emphasis added).

He was as serious about leading people out of "spiritual" bondage as he was about leading them out of social and economic disadvantage and exploitation. To Gene Smathers, a "gospel" proclaimed in words alone without any "practical action" related to people's "down-to-earth needs" was an incomplete gospel. So was a "gospel" that dealt solely with humankind's eternal salvation but did nothing about their earthly existence. Worse than that, he thought, were those who "bought into" a gospel of an angry God and salvation by fear. One of his most tenacious opinions was that those who chose to proclaim the Good News of the New Testament in this manner were in bondage to a false gospel.

In a charge to a congregation, used several times, Smathers said, "It is as the church goes out, not to exploit the world for the church's membership or prestige, but to serve the world without thought of return or reward . . . that the Gospel is truly proclaimed in the language of deeds and its message begins to get across to a world that thinks *it has no need for God.*" One measure of how closely he kept up-to-date with current themes in theology was that later, when the "Death of God" movement was in its ascendancy, he ended that statement with the words, "To a world that thinks *God is dead*"[8] (emphasis added).

This "conviction" continued throughout his ministry. It finds expression in one of the last sermons he ever preached. Entitled "Called to Creative Compassion" and based upon Isaiah 58: 6–12, it was composed in September 1967, during his moderatorial year and delivered at least two dozen times that year. At the dramatic climax of that sermon, Smathers said, "We are called, as God's people, to get down with the oppressed where they are and together with them seek constructive ways of dealing with their real problems and needs. The call to creative compassion is not a call to more 'religion,' but to a love of neighbor, a self-identification with him, which leads to the pursuit of justice and the actual meeting of his down-to-earth needs."[9]

The Christian community Gene Smathers envisioned was one in which the church would be characterized by love, grace, forgiveness, and freedom, and further, the church would engage the world through "practical actions"—actions that would touch all areas of community life. It was not one in which the church went out into the community to convert all the "sinners" to church membership. It was rather a community in which the church reached out in service to convince people of the love and grace of Jesus Christ. The church would go out into the community to serve all the families and individuals there in all their needs.

It was a community in which the pastor of the church, supported by his congregation, served as pastor to all people in the community and not just to those who were church members. It is a telling fact that all the programs that grew out of the church at Big Lick, especially the health service and the homestead project, served more people who were nonchurch members than it did those who were members of Calvary Church. The church was servant to all those within its reach.

One mundane example of how such love and grace were delivered to the whole community was the Calvary Church children's Christmas gift program. During the time Gene Smathers was pastor at Big Lick, virtually every National Missions church in the Presbyterian denomination had a Christmas gift program for children. In many, if not most places, it was a *rewards* program—a Gospel of works program. Children who came to Sunday school and/or church regularly during the year were *rewarded* with a Christmas gift.

That was not the way it worked at Calvary Church of Big Lick. If you were a child member of a family that lived in Big Lick or if you went to the Big Lick School, you (and all your younger siblings) received a Christmas package. In 1952, when the Big Lick School was consolidated and took in children from three other communities, the number of Christmas gift packages grew from around 50 to over 120. There were more non-attenders of Calvary Church, including some whose families attended other churches, who received gifts than there were children who attended Calvary Church. It was an *awards* program, a matter of grace and love. If you lived in Big Lick or went to the Big Lick School, or were in any way a part of the Big Lick community, you and all your siblings were *awarded* gifts.

However, he had other concerns for his parish. "Believing that to be Christian, we need to be freed from the bondage of provincialism and prejudice," Gene Smathers wrote in 1951, "every opportunity has been taken to have visitors from other regions, from other races and lands. This has borne fruit in a growing awareness that not every brother in Christ has a white skin or speaks American English."

Earlier in that article, he said, "Gratitude to God and to others has been the basis . . . of a continuing concern for all God's Children. It was not difficult to secure the interest and support of church and community for bringing a displaced (DP) family from Hungary to Big Lick, and for other projects for overseas relief."[10]

At the end of that article, he wrote, "Moses never reached Canaan, and here we will never reach ours, but the journey has been thrilling and worthwhile. And we have come to know that, despite our unworthiness and weaknesses, the power and grace of God are adequate for every need and situation. If only we had greater faith!"[11] (Notice that in his articles, speeches, and lectures he never uses the singular *I*, but always the plural *we*. That was the nature of how he thought about the church.)

He never abandoned the vision of building a Christian rural community, although the details of it changed from time to time as both Big Lick and the world around it changed. This vision was at the core of his understanding of the Gospel, and it was part of what kept him in Big Lick all those years. At some point, he decided that creating and sustaining such a community was a lifetime endeavor and could not be accomplished if leaders changed every few years.

The largest single influence on Smathers's thinking came not from a theologian, but from a church administrator. Cast like Elijah's mantel over Elisha (1 Kings 19:19), the wisdom and writings of Warren Hugh Wilson fell with particular power on Gene Smathers. Smathers called Wilson's little booklet *The Second Missionary Adventure*,[12] the most influential book he ever read. Only thirty-two pages long, it was never intended to be a book at all. It began life as the 1915 Annual Missionary Address at Oberlin College. It was published at the insistence of some of Wilson's friends.

In his address turned booklet, Wilson argued that it was time for the church to expand its role from merely saving individual souls to saving communities and neighborhoods. He believed that the church was a social as well as a divine institution and, as such, had a role to play in the redemption of communities as well as individuals.

Wilson ended his address/booklet by saying, "It is given to only a few to be the adventurers for God on the outer bounds of human order and progress and faith . . . who shall go out on [God's] creative experiments, in themselves uniting the gifts of the university with those of the church . . . Their service shall be for all mankind no matter how small the wayside pool they look into; no matter how remote the community they know and love, their story will be worth telling."[13]

It can hardly be doubted that Smathers saw himself as one of Wilson's "Second Missionary Adventurers." It was an adventure in which the church no longer served only as a center of worship and a place for individual conversions. It was rather a journey in which the church would be the center for all action in the community, a church that would serve the needs of all people within its reach and work to bring all aspects of community life within the redemptive purposes of God. No matter how small, the church would share the knowledge it was acquiring with people of all races and nationalities from all over the world, and reach out to serve oppressed and disadvantaged people wherever they might be. It was no accident that Big Lick hosted visitors from all over the United States and all over the world, hosted interracial work camps twenty years before the civil rights movement, sent relief boxes to Europe after World War II, and sponsored and helped settle a refugee family.

The first two theologians that influenced Smathers were his seminary professors, Julian Price Love and Lewis J. Sherrill. Love taught English Bible and was largely responsible for Smathers's lifelong orthodox interpretation of scriptures. Sherrill taught religious education (and was dean of the seminary). Sherrill is quite well known for his theology of religious education and its place in the life of the church.

It was in religious education that Gene Smathers finished at the top of his class, and Sherrill is largely responsible for Smathers's beginning theory of religious education. Smathers ended up at a somewhat different point than Sherrill, considering any subject (economics, cooperatives, health, recreation), which Christians studied together *as Christians* to be part of religious education. Any study that moved a community toward being a fully Christian community was religious education according to Gene Smathers.

The final purely theological influence on Smathers's thinking came from Reinhold Niebuhr and his promotion of "Neo-Orthodoxy" and "Christian realism." Smathers's emphasis on relating faith to the "real world," his advocacy of racial and labor justice, his leadership in experimenting with racial integration prior to the civil rights movement, the sponsorship of a refugee family after WWII, and his subscription to non-pacifistic "realism" with respect to politics and relations between nations all point to Niebuhr's influence.

He melded Niebuhr's thought together with bits and pieces from Reformed theologians (including Calvin), the church fathers (e.g., Augustine), and more than a spattering of activists/writers/ theologians such as Dorothy Day and the Catholic Workers movement, Walter Rauschenbusch and the social Gospel movement, William Stringfellow, Thomas Merton, and Henri Nouwen. Mixed in with this was his generally orthodox interpretation of the Bible. The final product was a theological framework that was firmly biblical, notably Niebuhrian, activist, eclectic, and never completely finished.

A devout Presbyterian, he adhered fairly closely to the orthodox Reformed position on most issues. However, he tried to make the churches he led as much community churches as possible and was not averse to bending some of the Presbyterian rules from time to time. On occasion, he practiced rebaptisms by immersion at the request of new people joining the church out of a Baptist background, and he had his own interpretation of the Presbyterian doctrines of election, predestination, and covenant theology. He did not believe that persons were predestined to hell, if he believed in hell at all.

He believed that God chose (called or elected) persons, but he did not believe that any person could know for sure if he or she was among the elect or not. The human capacity for self-deception and the power of sin were just too strong. All you could do was to take actions and see how they turned out. He could be very strict with respect to certain practices of the church, such as the time he severely scolded some preteen girls who were "baptizing" a cat in a rain barrel. He scolded them not for drowning the cat, but for profaning a sacred sacrament of the church.

He emphatically accepted most core beliefs of orthodox Protestant Christianity—the Divinity and Bodily Resurrection of Christ; the Trinitarian formulation of Father, Son, and Holy Spirit; salvation by grace; evangelism as the primary task of the church (though, as explained elsewhere, he had a slightly unorthodox interpretation of evangelism). He trusted and relied upon the authority of the Bible, not that it was inerrant or infallible, but that it was the one necessary and sufficient revelation of the Word made flesh and of what God intended for human beings to be and to do.

He took his ecumenism seriously and went further than most people are willing to go. Ecumenism meant cooperation with other churches even when he did not agree with the program they were promoting (such as a countywide revival). He worked hard to get fundamentalist Baptist and others who did not agree with him into the countywide Ministerial Association. But for him, ecumenism went much further than that.

Believing that no distinction could be drawn between sacred and secular, ecumenism included cooperating with "secular" agencies that were working for the health and well-being of individuals and the community. Once the church had satisfied itself that a secular agency was working for the "dignity, worth, and total well-being of persons," then he believed and taught that "the church . . . must realize that God is working through other than ecclesiastical channels to bring healing and wholeness into personal and community life, and [the church must] be willing to know and cooperate with its 'secular' allies."[14]

Smathers's thinking was too biblically based, and his foundational theology too nearly orthodox for him to be considered theologically "liberal" in the first third of the twenty-first century. Yet his insistence that love in action was the only effective means of evangelism and a "Christian community" the only faithful outcome thereof leave him little room on the "evangelical" or "orthodox" side of the fence either. Moreover, his political orientation was decidedly liberal, and according to his own "conviction" about the "unity of Life," his political orientation cannot be separated from his theological beliefs. He was God's own unique adventurer. He had a faith ("Christ is Lord of all life and love is the law of life"), a calling ("to serve poor rural people"), and a vocation ("practical action" or love in action). Those were all he ever asked for, and all he ever needed.

NOTES

[1] This was not an entirely accurate statement, though he often claimed it. By his own definition of evangelism (to help people grow in their ability to love one another), he was quite successful. What his congregation may have lacked in size, it and the members thereof had built up their capacity to love one another and others. This is as much a part of the building up of the Body of Christ as is the growth in membership. Moreover, at the time of his death, active participation in his congregation was more than double what it was upon his arrival in the community. During his tenure, three times as many people had become members of his church as when he arrived, although many of them subsequently moved elsewhere. Also, his congregation had become much more diverse, including people from outside the Big Lick community and people with more formal education. Some of those came because of his sermons; others came because of the nature of the congregation.

[2] Eugene Smathers, "The Function of the Minister in Relation to Secular Culture," undated lecture. Published as "The Function of the Minister in Relation to Rural Culture," *The Christian Rural Fellowship Bulletin* 145 (September 1949), 2–3.

[3] Eugene Smathers, "On a Smaller Frontier," presentation at a "School of Missions" held at Second Presbyterian Church, Chattanooga, Tennessee, February 22, 1961, 5–6, 12–13.

See also Eugene Smathers, "The Church in Appalachia," *The Christmount Voice* 12, no. 4 (April 1964), 1 and 4. Except in this article, he is trying to convince others that the church must have these same convictions if they are to have an effective ministry in Southern Appalachia.

[4] Eugene Smathers, "A Rural Church Program that Makes Religion the Qualifying Factor in Every Experience of Life," a paper presented at the Seventh Annual Meeting of the Christian Rural Fellowship

held at Nashville, Tennessee, October 22–23, 1941. Later published in *The Christian Rural Fellowship Bulletin* 66 (November 1941), 1–8.

5   Eugene Smathers, "The Characteristics of a Christian Rural Community: The Big Lick Community, Tennessee," *The Christian Rural Fellowship Bulletin* 61 (April 1941), 1–5. (This article was a_prize-winning essay in a contest conducted by the Christian Rural Fellowship on the subject "What Are the Characteristics of a Christian Rural Community?")

6   Ibid, Smathers, Characteristics of a Christian Rural Community.

7   Eugene Smathers, "My Call from God," *The New Century Leader*, November 1951. An expanded and slightly different version of this article appeared in the November 4, 1951, David C. Cook Young People-Adult Sunday school lesson material.

8   Material contained in Gene Smathers's papers and notebooks.

9   Eugene Smathers, "Called to Creative Compassion," sermon composed and delivered several times in 1967.

10 Smathers, "My Call from God," op. cit.

11 Ibid, My Call

12 Warren Hugh Wilson, *The Second Missionary Adventure*, originally published by the Fleming H. Revell Company, New York, 1915. Republished by Nabu Press, Charleston, SC, as a public domain document, date unknown.

13 Ibid, Wilson, 31–32.

14 Eugene Smathers, "The Church in Appalachia," *The Christmount Voice* 12, no. 4 (April 1964), 4. The same material is mentioned in numerous other places in his papers.

CHAPTER 18

THE ROAD LESS TRAVELED

On the Practice of Ministry

> *His gifts were that some should be apostles, some prophets, some evangelists, some pastors and teachers, to equip the saints for the work of ministry, [and] for building up the body of Christ.*
>
> —Ephesians 4: 11–12

"I had come to remain as long as I could be of effective service in building a Christian rural community."[1] These words from early in the very first article Gene Smathers ever wrote about his ministry in Big Lick set the foundation for his practice of ministry. The ending sentence in that same article provided the remainder of the framework. In the last paragraph of that article, he outlines some of his basic beliefs that he thought might have been distorted by something he had written earlier in the article. He ends by writing, "I expect I have only added confusion in my attempt to clarify my faith, for *my vocation is practical action rather than philosophical reasoning.*"[2] The building of Christian community by practical actions is what he became known for and what got him elected as moderator of the 179th General Assembly of the United Presbyterian Church.

Gene Smathers became a rural National Missions pastor through his sense of calling and because he had a vision. He never went to school to be (and when he was in school he never thought he would become) a church construction foreman, a carpenter, a mason, a rural health care advocate and pioneer, an economic developer, a land reformer, a surveyor, a tree farmer, a forester, a race relations pioneer prior to the civil rights movement, a demonstration farmer, a farm labor organizer, a soil conservationist, or a prophet railing against the destruction of the soil and other natural resources or lamenting the injustice toward the tenants and sharecroppers who worked the land or lambasting the human failure to till and tend the earth according to God's will. Nor did he study to be a tour guide, a refugee resettlement agent, or a parole officer.[3] He taught himself to be all these other things because he believed them essential to his role as pastor and to his pilgrimage toward fulfillment of that vision, which he discovered was always just beyond his grasp, the building of a fully Christian rural community.

"The good pastor," he wrote in an article on the function of the minister, "must identify his life with that of his people, and *by his people I mean all within the community of his ministry and not just those on the membership roll of his congregation*. Out of identification will come the desire to bring the riches of God's grace into the life of his people and their community"[4] (emphasis added). In this statement, Smathers sets forth the two things other than his own personal attributes that caused "his people" to love him so much. First, there was the matter of identifying with the people to whom he was ministering, and secondly, there was his definition of who constituted "his people."

His identification with his people (meaning everyone in the community he served) could hardly have been more complete. It began with the attitude he brought with him to his ministry. Virtually all the agencies and programs that came into the Southern mountains in the first half of the twentieth century, including the churches (and all those that followed them such as the New Deal and War on Poverty programs of the 1930s and 1960s), had as their purpose to change rural mountain people.

One of their oft-stated goals *was* "to bring the mountaineers into the American mainstream." One of the churches' unstated goals was to "save" or "convert" the heathen hillbillies. This was not so with Gene Smathers. He believed that the rural mountaineers' values and way of life were superior to those of the urban American mainstream. He believed that all the mountain folk needed was more economic opportunity, the ability to make a living while maintaining their way of life.

The less urbanized the rural mountain folk were, the better he liked it. This was unquestionably a romantic notion. It discounted both the lure of things urban and the wishes of rural people themselves to partake of the things that urbanization provided. By the midpoint of his ministry in Big Lick (c.1950), he had recognized that Big Lick was not going to remain rural forever in the way it had been. Thereafter, he changed his modus operandi. He turned his attention to the development of nonfarm jobs, health care, and other services in the larger community centered in the county seat of Crossville. In Big Lick, he tried to help the people hang on to some of their rural values and way of life as they became more and more urbanized.

His identity and solidarity with "his people" included dressing as they did—in plain work clothes when he was home during the week and in a simple suit for Sunday mornings. He spoke the language of rural people, appreciated and laughed at their sense of humor, and adopted the mannerisms and customs of the Big Lick folk. Outside the community, he was often addressed as "Reverend" or "Brother" or later (after he received an honorary doctorate) as "Doctor" or another of the titles by which ministers are set apart from laypeople. However, he was never addressed that way by members of his community. At his insistence, he was addressed simply as "*Mr.* Smathers" (the way all adult men of respect were addressed in the Big Lick of his generation).

He was six feet tall, 150 pounds of steely muscle and bone. He had the hands of a working man—hard, weather-beaten, and calloused.

He was physically strong for his size, the result of years of work on his parents' farm, the Calvary church farm, and his own one hundred acres that was scrubby woodland when he and Loucile bought it. Throughout his life, he maintained the demeanor of a farmer, loved to see things grow, and was a master gardener and farmer. As expressed in a classic country song, "He was country, when country wasn't cool."

He went to the community with some advantages in these matters. He was born and reared on a farm. He understood and loved rural people. He knew how to talk about rural topics. He grew his own vegetables and butchered his own hogs just like others in Big Lick did. He jumped in to help neighbors with difficult chores just as he accepted their help when he needed it.

But it was the extension of this identification into his pastoral ministry—praying with people; helping bury their dead; serving as a pallbearer; taking them to the doctor; quietly reading scripture to the dying; sitting up with them when they were sick; visiting with them on their front porch; advising them in his low-key way of more productive farming methods; helping fill out tax and Selective Service forms; making loans from the church homestead project when they needed repairs to their existing house or a new home, or in some cases just when they needed a means of transportation; suffering with them through family tragedies; and trying to help them find solutions to their most-pressing needs. It was these that made his ministry work. Hardly a day passed that he was not helping someone with something.

"Lord, how I loved that man." Words spoken of Gene Smathers forty-five years after his death by one who had been a member of his congregation but whose other family members had not been. He came to be loved by "his people" (and not only church members) not just because of his self-identification with them and not only because they experienced his love themselves, but also because they had seen his love at work among those who were not church members (though they were often relatives of church members). That was what made Gene Smathers unlike any other minister they had ever known.

No matter how poor they were, he never treated "his people" as objects of charity. A benevolent but paternalistic "tall steeple preacher" once wrote him to criticize the fact that some of the old clothing which that minister's church was sending to a certain Mrs. Hale, a member of Smathers's congregation, was being sold rather than given away. In reply, Smathers wrote,

> To my knowledge Mrs. Hale has never sold any of the things . . . sent to her. This vindicates her. But I would like to go a step further . . . As pastor I receive a good many boxes of used clothing, and we have found it best to sell this clothing at a very small price, allowing those who do not have money to work for them . . . I know many communities which have been pauperized by the very thing which you are demanding. *Charity . . . can be a dangerous thing to the character of those receiving it.* We have felt that the self-respect of our people should be conserved.[5] (emphasis added)

That statement captures his opinion of charity.

Humble and self-effacing, he laughed a lot, often boisterously and frequently at himself. Determined, dedicated, dependable, disciplined, and focused on a vision, he was a natural leader. He was outgoing and loquacious. He enjoyed people and a good honest discussion (read: "argument") from time to time. Confident but not haughty, he was unafraid of failure, willing to try new things, even when he suspected they might fail. He even thought that God sometimes might call a person to a task at which he or she would fail.

With the exception of the church itself and the Calvary Church Homestead Project, all the initiatives he undertook at Big Lick died before he did. He saw it simply as the death-to-life cycle of all living things—man-made things as well as the flora and fauna of the natural world. The death of the Big Lick health program helped to start a hospital and broader health services in the whole county. The death of the Big Lick Farmers' Association helped bring to life a countywide farmers cooperative that exists to this day. Other things died, however, with no successor. He took it as a challenge to lift his horizons and spend his energies on broader countywide social and economic efforts.

In thirty-six years of ministry, he prepared and delivered over 1,400 sermons without ever once repeating the same sermon to the same congregation. He was an average speaker and thought himself a poor preacher. His sermons were often long (too long for a twenty-first century audience) and delivered tepidly. But for those who could listen long enough (as many mid-twentieth-century people could), they found his sermons always well prepared, logical, often profound, and packed with practical down-to-earth suggestions for actions to be taken.

His sermons were often laced with evidence of his scholarly research. He let his scholarship show through even among a people that never demanded such. In the beginning of his ministry, they were even a little suspicious of such scholarship in sermons. There were few rhetorical flourishes or clever phraseology, but he refused to "dumb down" his sermons although many members of his congregations had no more than a third-grade education. He respected their native intelligence, and they came to understand and appreciate his sermons. Several of his sermons stood up well when delivered to large sophisticated urban audiences when he was on tour or at various places during his year as moderator of the general assembly. Maybe that is all that needs to be said of Gene Smathers as a preacher.

An active churchman beyond his congregations, he often served as chairman of the National Missions or Ministerial Relations Committee of his presbytery (crucial committees in a presbytery in which 80 percent of the churches were National Mission churches). In such roles, he was often asked to speak at the ordination or installation of a new pastor. He would share (as he said) not a "charge," which he considered "presumptuous," but "simply a few convictions regarding the nature of the ministry to which both you and I have been called."[6]

Among these "convictions," which he repeated in longer lectures he was often requested to deliver to collections of ministers, was that one needed to dismiss the words "success" and "successful." Saying that neither they nor any of their connotations are found anywhere in the New Testament, he substituted the words "faithful," "effective," and "worthy." He insisted that in these terms, a pastor could be "faithful and effective even in a tormented or dying or insecure community."[7]

In these lectures/articles, "non-charges," and talks, he went on to say,

> God judges our worth as pastors, our "success" if we must use that word, not by the abilities we possess, or the prestige we achieve, or the size of the church we serve, but by the fullness of our vision of what He is calling us to be and do, and by our faithfulness to that vision . . . The ministry of Christ is the pattern for our ministry, and it took the form of a servant, coming to climax on a cross . . .
>
> The ministry of Jesus was the concrete expression of *who* he was. *Being* was prior to *doing* . . . His Lordship was an acceptance of powerlessness, a willingness to sacrifice one's own interest, a being available for others, forgetfulness of self and love for one's fellows . . . Our authority . . . does not reside in our personal endowments or the quality of our Christian piety or in our supernatural wisdom . . . but solely in our function as witnesses to Jesus Christ, to who he was, to what he said, and to what he did and is doing.[8]

He often cited Ephesians 4: 11–12 and wrote, "Each [pastor] is to be measured by how he uses his particular gift or gifts 'for the equipment of the saints for the work of ministry [and] for building up the body of Christ'" (Ephesians 4: 12).

He continued later, "A second point of emphasis is most important, and it is this: not the pastor alone, but the whole church is minister. Therefore, the pastor is successful not by building a self-serving institution, making raids into enemy territory -- the secular world – and rescuing souls for security in a sacred fortress –the church– but to the degree that he devotes his talents intelligently and energetically toward equipping the people of God for their service in the world."⁹ How did these principles work out in his own practice of ministry? His congregation (and many of "his people" outside the church) came to embrace his definition of the Gospel (Christ is the Lord of *all* life; love is the law of life; the church, as the servant people of its Servant Lord, does not exist for itself but must minister through "practical actions" to all people within its reach in the wholeness of their lives). His congregation became the servant church he envisioned as central to a Christian rural community.

His congregation (and many of "his people" outside the church)— all indigenous residents of a small white Southern community— came to judge people on the content of their character and not the color of their skin or the language they spoke. They demonstrated this by hosting, at some risk to themselves, the first interracial work camps in the rural South, dozens of foreign visitors, and a displaced-persons family after World War II.

His congregation (and many of "his people" outside the church) became willing to risk up to 20 percent of their annual income to improve the welfare of the whole community. Gene Smathers's account of this process and his claim that it too constituted "religious education" is recorded elsewhere in this book (see chapter 6).

His congregation supported a recreation program for young people in spite of severe criticism by neighboring ministers. In a forum on "religious education," Gene Smathers wrote of his understanding of the religious education dimension of this issue:

> A small rural community was to have its first real church building. There was a desire to have a . . . social hall and kitchen. The question arose, "Why does a church need these things?", thus giving a natural situation for a meaningful discussion of what constitutes an adequate program for a rural church . . . A program of recreation was being developed by this church and the problem of overcoming prejudice and of developing a positive attitude toward play offered many

opportunities for religious education. These incidents are related simply to indicate the rich possibilities available for a vital program of religious education in the simplest concerns of rural community life.[10]

His congregation elected a woman as elder in1933 (twenty-three years before the first woman was *officially* ordained as an elder in the Presbyterian Church [USA]). Then again in 1956, the year in which Margaret Towner supposedly became the first woman *officially* ordained as an elder in the Presbyterian Church (USA), the Calvary Church congregation elected its second woman elder. Also, in 1959, a woman who grew up in the Big Lick Church (Smathers's daughter) graduated from seminary with a BD degree—one of the first women in the Presbyterian Church to do so and nine years before that denomination officially sanctioned the ordination of women as ministers. As in many other things, the Big Lick congregation was ahead of its time.

In 1965, an interviewer from *Teens* magazine asked Smathers, "You say you've been here for thirty-one years? That's a long time! Don't you feel that you are kind of wasted, being in such a little place for so long?"

Smathers replied,

> No, I really don't. A great churchman of former years told of the biology professor who sent him to study life in a barnyard pond. There he discovered the greatness and significance of what seems very small. A wise philosopher said, "the more a man belongs to his own times and community, the more he will belong to all times and all countries." The best contribution the average Christian can make to the cause of Christ is to do what he can in the local place where he lives and labors. And even though it be a small place, it can have value for the wider world. *It is not the size that matters, but what happens to persons. And experience here indicates that something important happens to persons when any group of people, however small and obscure, in a common devotion to Jesus Christ, seek to relate the gospel to the whole of their lives.*"[11] (emphasis added)

A lot of what happened to persons through Gene Smathers's pastorate and other initiatives was that they gained confidence in themselves. They came to realize that with a little help, they could solve their own problems. They developed a tremendous core of leadership. A dozen or so indigenous leaders not only made the Big Lick endeavors successful, but later emerged from one of the most remote communities in the county to assume leadership positions in countywide organizations. The development of indigenous leaders and the development of personal and community self-confidence were two of the objectives Gene Smathers set out to achieve. Smathers once wrote, "The essential thought of the [Big Lick] story [is] the breaking down of the walls of despair, defeat, [outmoded] tradition, etc."[12]

The building of the church was important for two reasons: First, Gene Smathers believed that the church should be at the center of all efforts to improve people's lives, spiritually, materially, recreationally, and however else. Secondly, by beginning with something, the building of a church that both he and they greatly desired, he was able to generate sufficient interest and energy to accomplish a significant task. And they built not just any church building, but a building that was when it was built and still today is considered by many to be the most beautiful church building in Cumberland County. This gave them confidence to try other things, and it grew from there.

He left a church which has never locked its doors, but so respected in the neighborhood that it has never been vandalized.

There was a certain dichotomy in the man. On the one hand was the scholar who "loved books" and could "never have enough of them," one who never tired of the discipline of reading and research. On the other was the activist pastor who claimed repeatedly, "My ministry is one of practical action not philosophical reasoning." There is a certain stark contrast in those two statements, and those contrasts existed in the man. The only one of three siblings to attend college, he became the consummate scholar who read voraciously, wrote articles and pamphlets, lectured widely, and for three years headed the Department of Church and Community at Vanderbilt University Divinity School.

On the other hand was the practical down-to-earth practitioner who believed and practiced that all the knowledge in all those books was not worth a "hill of beans" unless it resulted in "practical actions" that brought people closer to God and to the fuller, more abundant life promised in Christ. At the same time, he knew that such "practical actions" did not spring up sui generis but were the result of study and mastery of the knowledge found in those books.

He claimed that his vision of a Christian rural community was always just beyond his reach and that he, like Moses, would never reach that promised-land. However, judging from his letters, papers, and journals, and the testimony of those who knew him well, on two occasions, Gene Smathers came close to realizing his dream of creating a Christian rural community as he understood it. It happened first in 1934–1941 and again in the mid-1950s. The details of such a community were different in the1950s than in 1934–1941, but by his light, he felt close to his goal at those two times. The first time was waylaid by World War II, and the second by the outmigration of Big Lick folk to Northern cities in search of better-paying jobs. Thus, it remained true—his goal was always just beyond his reach. And maybe that is just the way God intended it to be.

NOTES

1. Eugene Smathers, *"I Work in the Cumberlands,"* pamphlet published by the Fellowship of Southern Churchmen in 1940. Also published in *Rural America*, The American Country Life Association Inc., vol. 18, no.7 (October 1940), p. 6 in the pamphlet; p. 4 in the *Rural America* article.
2. Ibid, Smathers, "I Work in the Cumberlands," 14 in Pamphlet, 7 in *Rural America* article
3. Among other things, he negotiated an arrangement with the Department of Corrections whereby a man who had been convicted of second-degree murder was paroled into his custody and oversight, thereby making him the man's parole officer (because the man's family needed a husband and a father).
4. Eugene Smathers, "The Function of the Minister in Relation to Secular Culture" (his title); "The Function of the Minister in Relation to Rural Culture" (publication's title), *The Christian Rural Fellowship Bulletin*, no. 145 (September 1949), 1–8.
5. Eugene Smathers, letter to the Reverend Russell Paynter, DD, pastor of the Bethany Temple Presbyterian Church, Philadelphia, Pennsylvania, June 24, 1940.
6. Eugene Smathers, "Charge to Pastor," Eugene Smathers papers.
7. Eugene Smathers, "How to Be a Successful Pastor," (title assigned), lecture to the Annual Ministers' Conference of the Cumberland Presbyterian Church, January 1965.

   Also published in *Town and Country Church*, no. 185, (Nov.–Dec. 1965), 10–14. (Regarding the contemporaneous nature of his reading and research, seven of the twelve references cited in the above lecture/ article were published in the preceding two years, and none were more than nine years old.)

Essentially the same material is found in Smathers's "Charge to Pastor" and "Charge to Pastor and People," Eugene Smathers papers.

8   Ibid, Smathers in articles and other papers cited immediately above.
9   Ibid, Smathers in articles and other papers cited immediately above.
10 Eugene Smathers, "Religious Education and the Spiritual Values of Rural life," *Religious Education* 40, no. 2 (March–April 1945): 74.
11 "An Interview with Eugene Smathers," *Teens*, Board of Christian Education of the United Presbyterian Church in the USA, 17, no. 4 (July–September 1965): 13. See also Eugene Smathers, "Ministry in Big Lick, Tennessee," *Counsel*, Board of Christian Education of the United Presbyterian Church in the USA, 17, no. 4 (July–September 1965): 27.
12 Eugene Smathers, letter to John Clark Rose, January 12, 1947, p. 2.

CHAPTER 19

"REFLECTIONS IN A DAY OF TROUBLE"

This also happened in 1957.

But now thus says the Lord, he who created you, O Jacob, he who formed you O Israel: Fear not, for I have redeemed you; I have called you by name, you are mine. When you pass through the waters, I will be with you, and through the rivers, they shall not overwhelm you; when you walk through the fire you shall not be burned, and the flame shall not consume you. For I am the Lord your God, the Holy One of Israel, Your Savior.

Soon or late a day of trouble, a day of personal and family distress and sorrow comes to us all . . . . Sooner or later [suffering] tracks out our footsteps and discovers our hiding places.

With those two quotations, one from Isaiah 43: 1–3 (RSV), the other from Wheeler Robinson, Gene Smathers began a sermon on September 15, 1957, one week after a delicate and dangerous surgery saved the life of their daughter Pat. This was not the Smatherses' first experience of sitting by a child's bedside as the child hovered between life and death. The previous occasion had turned out badly.

Twenty-one years previously, they had sat by the bedside of a sick child as he lay suspended between life and death. Their first son, Charles, had acquired pneumonia. Such was serious enough for any child, but this particular child had a defective heart valve—a "blue baby," they called him.

This time it was Pat, their only daughter and oldest child, who was lingering between life and death. She lingered longer than perhaps necessary because her doctors, some of the most reputable pulmonary specialists in East Tennessee and her family physician (a whiz-bang diagnostician) could not agree on a diagnosis. Her local doctor thought she had a tumor at the base of her trachea. The pulmonary specialists were convinced she had some object lodged in her windpipe. (It finally turned out that her family physician was correct).

She entered Fort Sanders Presbyterian Hospital in Knoxville on September 3, 1957. Upon further X-ray examination, it was determined that the object had grown considerably in the week since she was x-rayed in Crossville. The object was indeed a tumor, and it was growing rapidly. A tumor presented more complications for removal than a foreign object. The pulmonary specialists had never seen anything like it nor could they find any reference to a similar condition in any literature or references. Pat almost smothered to death twice as the doctors pondered how to conduct the surgery that was necessary to save her life. Part of the issue was, how does one keep the patient breathing (and not breathing in blood) while the windpipe is cut to remove the tumor?

This time, Gene's reaction was different than it had been with Charles's death. There was no talk of a loss and a gain, but only the sinking feeling of a potential loss. When Gene left home on September 4, heading for Knoxville and Pat's bedside, he embraced his son, Mike, and said with tears in his eyes, "I'm afraid she won't make it." It is the only time Mike ever remembers being embraced by his father.

On September 6, 1957, the four top chest surgeons in East Tennessee entered Pat's chest cavity through an opening in her back, removed the tumor, and inserted a stint in her windpipe to strengthen it where they had cut it. The whole operation was filmed to be used for training in medical schools and for reference by other doctors who might face a similar situation. On Sunday night, September 8, Gene wrote to his mother:

> I will not take time to tell all about Pat's trouble tonight as I am pretty well exhausted. This has been the most difficult week Loucile & I have ever faced, for it was never sure that the operation could be done successfully & it had to be done to save Pat's life. We will still be concerned until we are sure the tumor was not a cancer & until Pat fully recovers.

The tumor was not cancerous, and Pat did finally recover although it took her the better part of two years to do so. Fifty years later, she coughed up the spring-like stint that had been inserted into her windpipe during the operation.

One week after the operation, Gene Smathers faced his congregation and commenced his sermon as noted at the first of this chapter. He continued in that sermon as a pastor and educator, saying, in part,

> An age-old question which always comes with the day of trouble is the question "Why?" . . . There is nothing wrong or sinful in asking "Why?" . . . The heart of the Christian faith is not an intellectual formula for the universe and the mysteries of human life, but a strong trust that no matter what comes - comfort, adversity, or suffering, life or death - we are eternally safe with God . . . .

> In our recent day of trouble, when we confronted the real possibility that Pat's life could not be saved, [the] conviction that the fulfillment of one's destiny - to become, as a person, the best that is possible . . . is not entirely dependent on length of life - this conviction was a source of comfort and strength. [Pat's] twenty-three years had been full, she had become a person of integrity and maturity - and this was

more important than the number of years . . . We need always remember there are worse things than physical death - as Jesus put it: "do not be afraid of that which can kill the body, but fear that which can destroy the person!"

As the long hours dragged by, awaiting an outcome which was never certain, a conviction at a still deeper level sustained and gave peace in the midst of tears - the conviction, born of the Gospel, that God does not stand aloof from us . . . Instead, he comes right into the midst of our human experience, in Jesus Christ, . . . He comes to serve, to forgive, to strengthen and help, and He attaches no condition to his offer except our acknowledgment of need. And such an acknowledgment is not difficult when one stands helpless before the threat of death.

[Consider the scripture from Isaiah]. Here is no promise that those who trust God will escape the storms and fires of life, no promise of freedom from a day of trouble, no suggestion that the circumstances will be made less terrible. But there is the assurance of His presence and His concern, and herein lies the difference. His presence is a conviction, not a feeling - for in the midst of the flood or the fire, these may be all we can feel . . . God's promise is "I am with you," not "You shall feel me with you" - feelings come and go, surgings of hope and of despair, but the presence of God abides. The Christian faith bids us not to look in (to how we feel) but to look up. Our confidence in a day of trouble is not on man's changing moods but on God's fidelity, on His steadfast love . . .

So we see that the facing of suffering in faith may bring an increase in faith, and . . . point to another truth which some of us have discovered with new meaning in our day of trouble. This truth is this: nothing is lost when we make an offering of it. We can never lose a loved one whom we have committed to God's care . . . But if we endeavor to hold that

> loved one to ourselves - then we can lose that one and the loss is hell . . .
>
> The amazing truth is that the moment we let go, the instant we stop trying to push reality, life is enriched instead of being impoverished . . .
>
> Again it is through our days of trouble, of moments of suffering that we may come to a fuller understanding of the Cross. If this is so hard for me, to face the loss of my beloved child, how God must have loved you and me to give His only begotten son on Calvary's Cross . . .
>
> So may we interpret the unwelcome guest as the divine ambassador, and listen to his challenge, not as an unwelcome interruption to the pleasures of life, but as an invitation to rise to a higher level of living. The Cross is not an explanation but an invitation.[1]

The whole sermon is much longer and sprinkled with other passages of scripture, bits of folk wisdom, and quotations (with attribution) from books he had read. These excerpts are included here not only to show how he dealt with "the most difficult week" in his life, but also how he dealt with his congregation on the most difficult of subjects, namely, what does one do when God seems absent and evil seems triumphant.

"Gene and Loucile Smathers by their farm pond – 1967."

NOTES

[1] Eugene Smathers, "Reflections in a Day of Trouble," sermon preached on September 15, 1957.

CHAPTER 20

EUGENE SMATHERS REVISITED

A Man God Would Not Let Go

Briefly revisit with me those two times Gene Smathers felt like he came close to achieving his vision of a Christian rural community, 1934–1941 and the mid-1950s (take 1957 as an example). Call the first period the Big Lick Years and the latter the Cumberland County Years. From the time Gene and Loucile Smathers, with infant daughter, Pat, moved to Big Lick in 1934 until 1941, events moved along with the precision of clockwork and the speed of a runaway locomotive. Ten new initiatives in seven years. Gene Smathers was as busy as he could be with the work in Big Lick [See Chapter 14].

By contrast, in 1957, Gene Smathers was a member of the following countywide or regional organizations:

- member of the County Hospital Board
- chairman of the County Library Board
- an officer of the Cumberland County Farmers' Cooperative Board
- member of the United Fund Board
- member of the County Health and Welfare Committee
- member County Soil Conservation District Board 206

- member Cumberland County Planning Group Board
- member Hull-York Lakeland Conservation and Development Committee

At the same time, members of his Calvary Church congregation held ten (10) additional leadership positions in countywide organizations. In 1957, the following also occurred:

- Gene and Loucile Smathers faced "the most difficult time of our lives" with Pat's illness and near death.
- Gene Smathers faced and overcame the most serious "Communist/red-baiting" challenge of his life
- The Cumberland County Planning Group was planned and organized
- Gene Smathers was chairman and de facto Executive Secretary of the Fellowship of Southern Churchmen
- In presbytery, Gene Smathers served as chairman of the National Missions and Ministerial Relations Committees.

Looking at this remarkable record of achievement and service, the most crucial question still remains. Forensic investigators say that two apparent coincidences is one too many. Was it mere coincidence that after a frantic search Gene Smathers ended up in the *only* national mission field in the whole United States that was open in 1932? Was it coincidence that he and Loucile were married after much pleading by him one year earlier than they had planned? Was it coincidence that Gene Smathers—with his particular set of skills, his burning desire to serve rural people, and his unique vision of the future, along with his extraordinary wife, Loucile—ended up in Big Lick *precisely* at the moment when Carrie Murphy was retiring and when the leadership she had cultivated was ready to take the next step toward building a Christian community? He brought a vision, but had the people of Calvary Church and Big Lick not found that vision compelling, would

A PROFILE IN PURPOSE

they together have accomplished what they did? Was that, too, mere coincidence?

Even a skeptic would find this mound of coincidences to be rare and remarkable. Like the forensic investigator, a person of faith might say there are too many coincidences. It appears that Gene Smathers and Big Lick, Tennessee, were a match made in heaven. When so many apparent coincidences occur, a person of faith must ask, was this mere happenstance, or was there something more than mere coincidence at work here? Was perhaps the hand of God involved?

Gene Smathers with mountains in background, of which he said, "I like the mountains. They give me something to rest my eyes against."

APPENDIX 1

THE RADICALIZATION OF A COUNTRY BOY

> This section is included here as an appendix because it bears little relationship to the story of Gene Smathers and Big Lick, but it was a significant experience in the life of Gene Smathers.
>
> —The Author

CAWOOD, HARLAN COUNTY, KENTUCKY, MAY 13, 1931: Gene Smathers stepped off the train here about 3:00 PM today. He had finished his second year of seminary and was on his way to a summer placement in the coal town of Cawood with outposts in the Crummies Creek Coal Camp and Cranks, a farming community. At almost the same moment, forty-five other young men about his age disembarked from a train in Crummies. These were a contingent of the 370 National Guard troops the governor had dispatched to Harlan County one week earlier.[1]

Publically, the troopers' orders were to "restore order, protect lives and property . . . and to use all lawful means to rid the area of outside radical agitators."[2] The miners were promised that no strikebreakers would be allowed into the mines and that some of Sheriff J. H. Blair's

164 privately paid deputies (paid for by the coal companies) would be disarmed and discharged. The miners welcomed the troops with a Union band and two hundred miners marching and cheering.

The hope the miners placed in the Guardsmen was short-lived. It soon became apparent that the Guard's real purpose was to break the strike and get the mines reopened. None of the promises made to the miners were kept. The National Guard did have an immediate calming effect on the incendiary situation in Harlan County. Many miners' guns were confiscated, and the direct armed confrontations between miners and Sheriff Blair's deputies were eliminated. However, not a single deputy was disarmed or discharged, and strikebreakers were escorted into the mines by the troops.

The National Guard troops that arrived in Crummies on May 13 immediately commandeered the local school for housing; set up a machine gun on a railroad handcar; which they rode back and forth through the camp; collected all the miners' guns they could find; established martial law; broke up picketing; and the next day halted a march of three hundred miners on their way to picket the Crummies Creek mine.[3] Not that martial law of a sort did not already exist. Sheriff Blair had seen to that.

Blair told a reporter, "I did all in my power to aid the coal operators . . . Hell yes I issued orders to shoot to kill . . . That's what we use guns for here."[4] Miners did not experience much difference under the Guard's version of martial law than they had under that imposed by the sheriff. Miners told outside investigators, it was "no different working under the guns of the 'Tin Hats' and working under the guns of [Blair's] 'Thug' mine guards."[5]

Two days after his arrival, in his first letter home, Gene Smathers wrote his mother and family, "The soldiers are here. There was a union demonstration yesterday . . . Crummies is under martial law . . . My sympathies are with the laboring men, tho [sic] at present one has to watch his expression of his sentiments."

A PROFILE IN PURPOSE

In a way, he had asked for this. On April 16, he had written Warren H. Wilson of the Presbyterian Board of National Missions, asking for an assignment in the Eastern Kentucky coal fields. He explained that he thought it would do him good to be exposed to an industrial situation since he had never experienced one. On April 28, he heard that he had gotten the assignment. Neither he nor the board expected him to step into the midst of a labor war.

The Harlan County labor war of 1931 began in February when the coal companies cut wages by 10 percent to $0.33 per ton, far below what was being paid in other fields. In response, dozens of miners walked out, saying, "We'd rather strike and starve than work and starve."[6] Unorganized and unrepresented by any union, the striking miners were evicted from company housing and left to starve. Many of them moved to Evarts, a "free" (non-company) town where several local officials and merchants sympathized with the miners. In a few weeks, Evarts grew from a town of 1,500 to a teeming slum of over 5,000 people.

Early on the morning of May 5, a running gun battle between armed miners and fifteen of Sheriff Blair's deputies (all of them on coal company payrolls) broke out in Evarts. At least five men were killed and several others wounded. Harlan County went into a state of siege. Mines were shut down, schools were closed, and heavily armed sheriff deputies became the law. Asked what the law was, one miner's wife said, "The law is a gun thug in a big automobile."[7] One measure of who these deputies were is the fact that sixty-four of them were later indicted and twenty-seven convicted of felonies, eight for manslaughter and three for murder.[8]

On June 13, Smathers wrote home: "I suppose you have seen in the paper . . . about the killing here Thurs. nite [sic]. Mr. Chasteen ran a little restaurant [nearby], and we heard the shots and saw the soldiers carry him out . . . The man who killed him is an officer of some kind and a bad man in general. This is his seventh man . . . I suppose he will get out of this killing as easily as he usually does. He is hired by the operators as a mine guard . . . It sure gets my goat the way things are run in this county." [In fact, Bill Randolph, who killed Joe Chasteen, had killed four men previously, was a convicted felon, and was under another murder indictment when he was hired as a deputy. He was acquitted of Chasteen's murder.][9]

In his orders sending in the National Guard on May 7, the governor had said, "Several undesirable citizens from other states . . . are inciting and leading the troubles. Some are said to belong to societies called 'Reds' and 'Communists.'"[10] However, there was no evidence of Communist activity in Harlan County until June when the National Miners Union (NMU) began a food relief operation for starving miners and their families. They appeared only after both the more moderate United Mine Workers and the Red Cross had refused to provide such relief, the Red Cross under the contention that they did not intervene in an industrial dispute.[11]

Smathers had complained in his earlier reports to the board and in his letters home that neither Sunday school, church services, nor a Vacation Bible school could be conducted in Crummies because the soldiers were still housed in the school, the only building in the camp suitable for such activities. Then in his August report to the board, he wrote, "The work at Crummies has been completely blocked during the past month due to the wishes of Mr. L. P. Johnson, General Manager of the Crummies Creek Coal Company."

Mr. L. P. Johnson owned the Crummies Creek Coal Camp and everything in it. He owned the mine, he owned the houses, he owned the school, he owned the schoolteacher, and for all intents and purposes, he owned the National Guardsmen stationed there. He set the rules for the camp and had them enforced by the deputies (of which he was one) or the National Guard. Smathers would later call him a dictator.

Frances "Granny" Hager survived the battle of Evarts and most of the 1930s in Harlan and had the scars to prove it. She was later asked by oral historian Mike Mullins, "What was the roughest place over there . . . Roughest time you had here in organizing?" She thought a minute, then said, "Let's see. I'll think the name of the place—Crummies Creek . . . Now that was the roughest place we had in Harlan County."[12]

Within two weeks of his arrival in Harlan County, Smathers analyzed the situation there and the problem for the Presbyterian Church. In his first report from the field, dated May 26, 1931, Smathers wrote,

> It is hard for us to approach the people who suspicion [sic] that our sympathies are with the coal operators, and many of them do suspicion [sic] us. The fact is, however, that all my sympathies are with the laborers. The operators have this whole county tied up, and they control it as they see fit. It is a difficult task . . . to help folk become Christian when men that they know to be professing Christians oppress them and their families.

In his final report written in late August 1931, he wrote,

> "The problem at Crummies is keeping on the good side of the people and at the same time pleasing Mr. L. P. Johnson, general manager of the Crummies Creek Coal Company. He is able to prevent any religious work being done in the camp so it is necessary . . . to be in harmony with him. This is not always possible unless the worker ceases to think for himself and disregards his conscience . . . The environment around a mining camp where the camp boss is a dictator is not favorable.

Later in the same report, he writes,

> The problem at Cawood . . . is the attitude toward the Presbyterian Church . . . [The miners have] the idea that this church is for the 'high brows,' to use the phrase of the people themselves . . . It is my opinion that the [Presbyterian] Church will not be able to overcome this idea until it takes a fearless stand in regard to the labor situation . . . The Church

must not cater to the operators . . . and the masses must be able to see that the minister has their welfare at heart . . . *one of the greatest mistakes of our work this summer was our effort to remain neutral when neutrality is impossible* [emphasis added]. The church is in the community to serve as large a number as possible, and it should do so even at some cost to itself . . . The Cawood people are poor and the Church that serves them must have a poor man's outlook and a poor man's heart.

"The darkest places in Hell are reserved for those who maintain their neutrality in times of moral crisis."

Dante Alighieri
The Inferno

Smathers concludes his report by writing,

> There were many facts of interest that impressed themselves upon me this summer. The greatest of these was to see at first hand the result of the industrialization of a mountain community . . . [Also] of interest, as well as of disappointment, was the impotency of the church when faced with a trying industrial situation. The need for the Christianization of our industrial order has become very vivid since my first-hand experience in an industrial community.

As Florence Reece told the story, when the sheriff's deputies broke into her house in search of her husband, she tore a sheet off a calendar and wrote on the back of it what would become one of the best-known Union songs of all time: "Which Side Are You On?"[13] One verse makes the same point Smathers made in his report—in the Harlan County of 1931 neutrality was impossible.

When Gene Smathers left Harlan County, he knew which side he was on. As noted in his final report, he, like Reece, believed that neutrality in such a situation was an impossibility. He had witnessed the impotency not only of the church, but also of the moderate UMW and the Red Cross. He had seen that the Communist-led National Miners Union (NMU) and the left-leaning American Friends Service Committee were the only agencies with the courage and social platform that enabled them to provide food, clothing, and other relief aid to the out-of-work, stranded, and in some cases, starving miners and their families.

Smathers did not stay long enough to see the NMU turn their food and other assistance programs into a recruitment tool. They simply refused to feed or provide other assistance to a miner's family unless that miner joined the Communist Party.

Smathers had witnessed what happens when local law enforcement officers and the power of the state take their stand solely on the side of the mine companies and operators. He had witnessed firsthand at Crummies what happens when one man has dictatorial power over the lives of others. This had been Smathers's first exposure to the American "industrial order" of the 1930s. And it was not as if this was some isolated incident in the backwoods of Kentucky. The Harlan County mines and the Harlan County Coal Operators' Association were owned and controlled by some of the major American industrial corporations. J. P. Morgan's United States Steel Corporation, Samuel Insull's Peabody Coal Company, International Harvester, Henry Ford's Fordson Coal Company, the Mellon family of Pittsburgh, Detroit Edison, and others were the dominant forces in the Harlan County coal fields and masters of the greater part of Harlan County's 18,000 miners.[14]

Smathers had witnessed children and whole families literally starving to death, terror and violence used to intimidate not only miners but also those who tried to render aid to miner's families (e.g., on August 11, an NMU soup kitchen at Evarts was dynamited and destroyed),[15] murder committed under the cover of the law, and dictatorial control over whole communities. Moreover, the rights of free speech and assembly had been abrogated by laws against "criminal syndicalism" and "banding and confederating."

He had been radicalized by the experience. Though he never spoke at a union rally, never provided any relief supplies to the miners (an act punishable by imprisonment or worse), never overtly supported the union, his "radical" views and sympathies did not go unnoticed by the Harlan coal operators including certain influential members of the Presbyterian Church.

Among Smathers's "radical" actions was that he had taken some young people camping in defiance of the spirit if not the letter of L. P. Johnson's order forbidding the church to work in Crummies. Smathers always claimed that the camping trip and his expressed desire that some aid be delivered to the starving children and wives of striking miners were the most radical actions he took that summer.

Nevertheless, shortly after he returned to seminary that fall, he was faced with charges from some influential members of the synod of Kentucky that he was a Communist or Communist sympathizer. They instigated an abortive effort to get him expelled from seminary. The extant written record is unclear exactly what part the synod executive, the Reverend George S. Watson, played in this effort. What is known is that Watson was not pleased with Smathers's activities in Harlan and Smathers always believed Watson was behind the effort to get him expelled from seminary.

This first (though not his last) encounter with red-baiting did nothing more than solidify Smathers's thoughts about the Christian position relative to the industrial order. His thinking about what he called "the Christianization of our industrial order" was not all that different from the platform of certain Christian socialists. For some time afterward, he toyed with Socialism, briefly joined the Socialist League for Industrial Democracy, and supported Socialist presidential candidate Norman Thomas.

He was lured away from his Socialist leanings by the New Deal and became an FDR Democrat. However, he never wavered from some of the insights and sympathies he developed that summer in Harlan. Though he never joined an industrial union, throughout his life he steadfastly opposed so-called "right to work" laws and supported the absolute right of workers to organize and bargain collectively.

One interesting sidelight that Smathers never learned that summer in Harlan was that one of the striking miners, one of those indicted for murder on trumped-up charges, was a certain Charlie Bradley. Bradley had come to Harlan from the small community of Big Lick, Tennessee. One year later, Smathers and Bradley's family would cross paths under far more favorable circumstances.

NOTES

[1] For the most part, the material in this section came from the following sources:

    i. Eugene Smathers's papers, letters (from and to Smathers), and reports written while he was in Harlan County or immediately after he left; letters to family; letters to Loucile of which only a few still exist. Among the things revealed in those that do exist is that Gene got lice sometime that summer and that Loucile was not too happy about him being in Harlan County.

    ii. Accounts of his summer in Harlan County Gene Smathers reported to the author.

    iii. The author's own knowledge of the 1931 Harlan County strike and aftermath, garnered from fifteen years of teaching Appalachian Studies, first at Lees Junior College in the Kentucky coalfields (1970–1974) and later in his work with the Southern Appalachian Leadership Training (SALT) program from 1974–1985. He was one of the first two college instructors to teach Appalachian Studies (a course now offered by practically every college and university in the region).

    iv. The author received some corroborating oral history information from Harlan County native, retired coal miner, and former National Miners' Union organizer, Tillman Cadle. These conversations happened at the Highlander Research and Education Center, New Market, Tennessee. Other corroborating information came from Rebecca "Becky" Simpson of the Cranks Creek Survival Center. Some of these conversations were also at Highlander and others at the survival center.

v. Other sources used are credited throughout the text and/or footnoted below.

2   John W. Hevener, *Which Side Are You On*, Board of Trustees of the University of Illinois, 1978, p. 47.
3   Eugene Smathers's recollections as told to Mike Smathers. Also Hevener, ibid., 48–49.
4   Ibid, Hevener 39, 41.
5   Ibid, Hevener 49.
6   American Civil Liberties Union (ACLU) report, *The Kentucky Miners Struggle*, dated May 1932, p. 5.
7   Hevener, op. cit., 40. Also in Alessandro Portelli, *They Say In Harlan County: An Oral History*, Oxford Oral History Series, Oxford University Press, 2011, 187.
8   Hevener, ibid, 49. Also Portelli, ibid, 187 (with slightly different numbers).
9   Michael Smathers, "Appalachian Studies Notes." Also in Portelli, ibid, 187 (with slightly different numbers), and ACLU, op. cit., 7 (with still different numbers).
10 Hevener, op. cit., 46, 48.
11 Ibid, Hevener 45–48; also ACLU, op. cit., 5.
12 Portelli, op. cit., 4–5, 229.
13 The author heard this story directly from Florence Reece during his Appalachian Studies days. Also Hevener, op. cit., 60–61. Also see Portelli, op. cit., chapter 9, "No Neutrals There," for more background on the impossibility of neutrality.
14 Hevener, op. cit., 4. Also ACLU, op. cit., 4.
15 Ibid, Hevener, 60; ACLU, 10.

www.ingramcontent.com/pod-product-compliance
Lightning Source LLC
LaVergne TN
LVHW041803060526
838201LV00046B/1113